must-see ROME

TERESA FISHER

D0040344

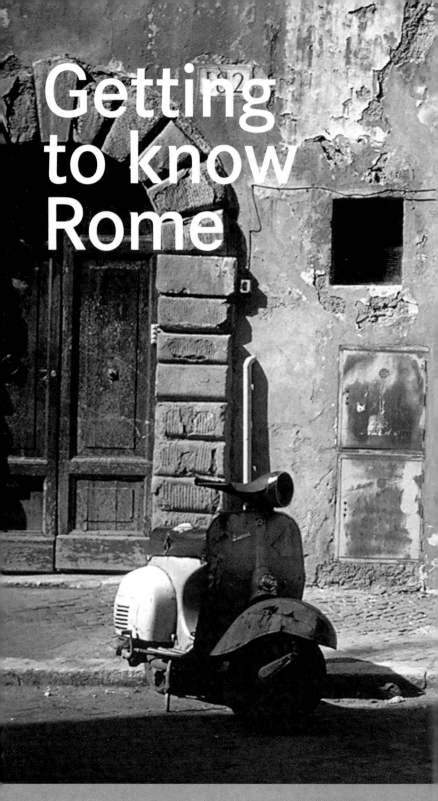

Getting to know Rome

must-see
ROME

CONTENTS

Published by Thomas Cook Publishing
PO Box 227, Thorpe Wood
Peterborough PE3 6PU
United Kingdom

E–mail: books@thomascook.com

Text: © The Thomas Cook Group Ltd 2000
Maps: © The Thomas Cook Group Ltd 2000
Transport map: © TCS 2000

ISBN 1 841570 400

Distributed in the United States of America by the Globe Pequot Press,
PO Box 480, Guilford, Connecticut 06437, USA.

Distributed in Canada by Whitecap Books, 351 Lynn Avenue,
North Vancouver, British Columbia, Canada V7J 2C4.

Distributed in Australia and New Zealand by Peribo Pty Limited,
58 Beaumont Road, Mt Kuring-Gai, NSW, 2080, Australia.

Publisher: Stephen York
Commissioning Editor: Deborah Parker
Map Editor: Bernard Horton

Series Editor: Christopher Catling

Written and researched by: Teresa Fisher

Cover photograph: John Heseltine

GETTING TO KNOW ROME

Discovering Rome

Rome wasn't built in a day, nor should it be visited in one. There are enough museums and monuments alone to last the average sightseer a lifetime, not to mention the ancient baths and temples, the triumphal arches, the churches, the seemingly endless galleries, the russet-coloured palazzi, the sun-baked piazzas, the fanciful statues, the fountains ... the list seems endless.

But with over 2,750 years of history and with such epithets as 'Seat of the Empire', 'Mother of Civilization', *Roma Dea* (The goddess Rome) and *Caput Mundi* (head of the world) – what else would you expect from the 'Eternal City', the City of Caesar, the city of *La Dolce Vita*?

Enjoyable chaos

That said, Rome is by no means a museum city carefully preserved in a vacuum as an *objet d'art*. Its inhabitants make this impossible, treating the grandeur of their inheritance with great nonchalance. Rome today is not about architecture or history. It's about the Romans themselves who give the city its distinctive character. Their maniacal driving, impassioned gesturing and noisy chatter animates the city or, according to some, renders it chaotic. Indeed, it is a city of surprising contrasts and contradictions: it is a modern capital set amid

ancient splendour, where Classical art competes for attention with haute couture; it has an extraordinary archaeological and architectural legacy to maintain, yet the traffic pollution is steadily eroding its treasures; it retains a rightful position as one of the world's top tourist cities yet faces all the problems of a major metropolis. Don't be alarmed therefore, if at first you find Rome disordered and unmanageable. In time you will start to appreciate that this perpetual hustle and bustle is a vital, dynamic facet of Rome's ever-evolving character as it struggles to incorporate the present into its eternal past.

Pace yourself!

So how to tackle the city? Of course, you must see St Peter's, the Pantheon, the Colosseum, the Sistine Chapel … but if you only have time for the major sights, you will miss the real Rome. Try to find time for simple pleasures. Get lost in the maze of terracotta and ochre streets that make up the ancient *centro storico* (historic centre), barter at the local market, linger over coffee in a hidden bar or hire a Vespa if you're feeling brave! Soak up the sun in a fountain-splashed square, stroll past the softly-illuminated 'sights' by night and notice the visible layers of history – ancient columns embedded in a Renaissance palazzo, an exuberant Baroque façade superimposed on a medieval church. Shop in some of Europe's chic-est boutiques, and be sure to try the local cuisine and wines that reflect a centuries-old culture.

If you take the time to absorb its special atmosphere, you will find that Rome will inspire the mind, appeal to the senses and capture the heart as no other city can. It's true, one lifetime is not long enough to know Rome. As Goethe so accurately observed, 'Rome is a world, and it would take years to become a true citizen of it. How lucky those travellers are who take one look and leave.'

A day in the life of Rome

Deep in their hearts the Romans appreciate more than any visitor the marvels of Rome, yet they appear to

take their city for granted. Daily, they pass ruined temples and triumphal arches en route to the office, they are used to sipping espressos beside a Baroque fountain in a piazza designed for chariot racing and toss their cigarette stubs into dustbins embossed with SPQR without a second thought for the centuries-old motto Senatus Populusque Romanus *(The Senate and the Roman People) which once adorned the legions' standards. Perhaps for this reason, modern critics read it as* Sono Porchi Questi Romani *(What pigs these Romans are).*

Familiarity breeds contempt

The Romans are not popular with their fellow countrymen. Hindered by an apparent lack of political direction and an obstinate bureaucracy, they are said to squander the money earned by the rest of the country, and to lay down laws for the country which they themselves ignore. There is an element of truth to these stereotypic accusations. As the travel writer Jan Morris remarked: 'Recession, pollution, crime and triple-parking seem to pass them by; if the city were suddenly Scandinavianised, all its buildings spick and span, all its traffic ordered, all corruptions cleansed, the Romans would hardly notice.'

Romans today

Nor are Romans noted for their piety, despite the presence of nine hundred churches and the Vatican, the spiritual and physical centre of Christendom. Only 3 per cent of the population goes to mass. As the local saying goes: 'Faith is made here but believed elsewhere.' They are, however, known for their zest for life, their good cheer and their *pazienza*. They are passionate, hot-blooded people who live life to the fullest – gesticulating constantly, honking their horns to celebrate weddings and football victories, pampering their children, gossiping in the local bar, and enjoying the hearty Roman cuisine to the full.

Mealtimes are a vital part of any day. According to Fran Lebowitz (*Metropolitan Life*): 'In Rome people spend most of their time having lunch. And they do it very well – Rome is unquestionably the lunch capital of the world.' Many people return home from the office to eat together as a family. Just before 1330, phone lines throughout the city get jammed as everyone phones home instructing the cook to *'Butta la pasta!'* (Throw the pasta on!). Watch how the roads then get grid-locked as everyone tries to reach their pasta while it is still *al dente*, followed by the essential afternoon *siesta*.

La bella figura

Romans are also renowned for their stylish albeit conservative dress sense and for spending a fortune on looking good. *La bella figura* – the art of looking, and being seen to look, one's best – is best observed during that excellent Roman ritual, the early evening *passeggiata*, when the entire population of the city promenades the streets to gaze in shop windows and to admire each other. Remember though, people-watching in Rome is not a spectator sport. For every person you watch, a whole crowd will be watching you so remember to dress and act accordingly. 'When in Rome . . .'

Yesterday and tomorrow

According to legend, the city started life as a small farming community founded in 735 BC by brothers Romulus and Remus (see page 25). It first developed into a noteworthy settlement under the Etruscan kings who built the first forum here. Gradually, the city spread to embrace the Seven Hills of Rome (see page 135), and eventually under the leadership of Julius Caesar and Augustus, it became the capital of the glorious Roman Empire. During the fifth century AD however, following waves of attacks from Visigoths, Vandals and Lombards, the Empire declined and in 476 the last emperor, Romulus Augustulus, was deposed.

🕯 *Waiting for an audience with the Pope*

Papal power

Before long the newly thriving papacy took over political and social control. By the middle of the eighth century the Lombards were defeated once and for all. They returned to the pontiffs a large region of central Italy which became known as the Papal States, with Rome as its capital. In medieval times, the city fell once more into decline, mainly due to power struggles between the Church, Rome's leading families and secular rulers. It did not fully recover until the late 15th century, when the papacy was restored to Rome from Avignon and the city once again triumphed as a source of learning and a leading centre for the arts. Today its many fine Renaissance and Baroque buildings stand as testimony to the power and influence of the pontiffs in shaping Western civilisation at this time. By 1870, when the Papal States joined the newly created kingdom of Italy, with Rome as its capital and Vittorio Emanuele as their king, the political power of the popes had already been restricted to the Vatican.

Il Duce and fascism

In 1922 Benito Mussolini's March on Rome and his seizure of power marked the start of over 20 years of Fascist rule in Italy. A spate of megalomaniacal building ensued, as a result of Mussolini's delusions of imperial grandeur and his desire 'to make Rome appear wonderful to the whole world, immense, orderly and powerful as she was in the days of the first empire of Augustus'. His processional routes – Via dei Fori Imperiali and Via della Conciliazione – are still the cause of controversy today. The Fascist era ended with the Allied liberation of Rome in 1943, and in 1946 the Italian Republic was established.

Into the Millennium

Today, the cobbled streets of Rome resound to the tramp of tourists coming to marvel at the remains of the city's 2,750 years of history, from the Classical remains of ancient Rome to the fascist office blocks of the 1930s. But Rome refuses to live in its past. As the Millennium rapidly approaches, a vast restoration project and a new building programme is under way. With record numbers expected to make pilgrimages to Rome and the Vatican during this Holy Year (*see page 89*), Rome's future as a major tourist destination, religious and cultural centre remains assured.

People and places

As former capital of the Roman Empire, capital of modern Italy and the headquarters of the Roman Catholic church, Rome has attracted many celebrities and famous figures.

Artistic mecca

For centuries artists and writers have been drawn to the sights of Rome: Italians Michelangelo, Raphael and Caravaggio in the early 16th century, French artists Nocola Poussin and Claude Lorraine in the 17th century, and Byron, Shelley, Keats, Goethe, Stendhal, Henry James and countless other celebrities during the Grand Tours of the 18th and 19th centuries (*see pages 102–103*). More recently, the famous Italian author Alberto Moravia (1907–90) was born in Rome, the setting for many of his novels.

The people's Pope

With the Vatican as the physical and spiritual heart of Catholicism, Rome abounds in priests, monks, nuns and church dignitaries who come to study at one of the Catholic centres. The city's most revered visitor was St Peter, Christ's

disciple, Rome's first bishop and guardian of the gates of Heaven, who became one of the early Christian martyrs, crucified upside down (as he felt unworthy of dying as Christ had) during the reign of Emperor Nero in AD 67. Since then, his successors have been considered Christ's representatives on earth. Today's Pope, John Paul II, is the first non-Italian pope since the 1520s. Son of an army officer, he read Polish language and literature at university and was a fine sportsman and actor. In order to continue his studies during World War II he worked in the stone quarries during the day, and studied by night. In 1942 (aged 22) he started to study theology in secret and was ordained in 1946. That same year he had his first collection of poems *Son of the Hidden God* published. A traditionalist Pope, today he exerts a tremendous influence on the lives of Catholics around the world (*see pages 152–153*).

Heads of state

As Rome is Italy's political capital, it is home to the head of state, the President of Italy. His offices are contained in the Palazzo del Quirinale (*see page 113*). In the past, Queen Christina of Sweden sought refuge here in the 17th century, as did James Edward Stuart following an unsuccessful attempt to win back the British throne. His son, Bonnie Prince Charlie, was born and died here. Napoleon came to Rome in 1797. His family continued to live here after his death in 1821, his notorious sister Pauline (pictured above) marrying into the great Roman Borghese family (*see pages 162–165*).

The beautiful people

Some of Italy's top designers are based in Rome, including Laura Biagiotti, (who finds inspiration in her medieval château on the outskirts of the city), the five Fendi sisters, (famous for their fashionable furs) and, most famously, Valentino, Rome's golden boy who rose to prominence during the *dolce vita* days of the 1950s and 1960s, with a clientele that included Sophia Loren, Jackie Kennedy and Audrey Hepburn. Look out also for tailors Battistoni, Gucci, Sorelle Fontana and Locatelli, who for years have dressed the city's élite in the finest of *haute couture*.

Getting around

Public transport

Do not be fazed by Rome's public transport system, which may initially seem chaotic, crowded and largely incomprehensible with its 234 different bus routes, 6 tram lines and metro network. It is actually very straightforward and will save you a lot of valuable sightseeing time if you are able to use it effectively.

Tickets

There are three main types of ticket:

B.I.T.

A *biglietto a tempo* or single ticket, valid for up to 75 minutes on all ATAC–COTRAL buses and trams, for one trip on the metro and for one trip on any metro-type main-line train (second class) within Rome.

C.I.S.

A *carta settimanale* or weekly pass, the same as the B.I.G. but valid for seven days.

Tickets must be bought before boarding any public transport from ATAC counters (Piazza dei Cinquecento, Piazza del Risorgimento, Piazza San Silvestro), tobacconists (*tabacchi*), news-stands and automatic ticket machines in metro stations. (Night buses are the exception to the rule, with a conductor on board selling tickets.) All tickets must be validated at the start of the first trip, in machines at the rear of buses and trams, at the entry gates of metro stations or in the entrance areas of rail stations. There are hefty on-the-spot fines if you are caught without a ticket.

Buses and trams

City buses and trams (run by ATAC) are orange and offer a cheap and frequent service between 0530 and 2340. Regional and suburban buses are blue (run by COTRAL). Bus

B.I.G.

A *biglietto giornaliero* or day pass, valid for unlimited metro, bus and train travel within Rome on the day that it is validated.

No. 590 is reserved for passengers with impaired mobility and follows the same route as Metro A, running every 90 minutes. Two electric minibuses (Nos. 116 and 117) shuttle people around the historical centre, passing many of the top sights. (During the evening, minibus No. 116 becomes No. 116T, operating a special theatre route before and after shows). A night bus service (*servizio notturno*, easily identifiable by the bus number followed by the letter N) operates 27 routes all over town between the hours of 0010 and 0530.

Work out your route, either by buying the official public transport map – *Roma Metro-Bus* – which contains detailed street plans, clearly marked transport systems and a booklet listing ticket prices and bus routes or by checking numbers and destinations at individual bus stops (*fermate*). Note that buses frequently have different return routes, due to the large number of one-way traffic systems. For further information contact ATAC at Piazza dei Cinquecento (*freephone 167–431784*). To use the bus or tram, enter by the back door, stamp your ticket (*see page 14*) in the machine at the rear of each bus or tram and leave by the centre door.

Useful bus routes:
Roman Forum and Colosseum: from Termini No. 64 to Piazza Venezia; from the Vatican No. 64 or 81; from Trastevere No. 60 or 170 to Piazza Venezia.

Pantheon, Piazza Navona and Campo de' Fiori: from Termini No. 64 or 492 to Largo Argentina; from the Vatican No. 64 or 62 to Largo Argentina.

Spanish Steps and Trevi Fountain: from Termini No. 492 to Via del Tritone; from the Vatican No. 62 to Via del Tritone; from Trastevere No. 60 to Via del Tritone.

Trastevere: from Termini No. 170 or 75 to Viale Trastevere; from the Vatican No. 23 or 280 to Piazza Gioacchino Belli.

The Vatican: from Termini No. 64; from the Colosseum No. 81; from Trastevere No. 23 or 280.

The Metro

Rome's Metro system is useful, safe and easy to master with two lines, that intersect at Termini. Line A links Cinecittà (southeast of the city) to Termini, the historic centre of Rome and the district of Prati near the Vatican. Line B links EUR (south of the city) with Basilica San Paolo, the Colosseum and the train stations of Ostiense, Termini and Tiburtina. Trains run daily approximately every 10 minutes from 0530 to 1130 (0030 on Saturday).

Useful metro stops to:
Vatican Museums – Line A: Ottaviano

Colosseum – Line B: Colosseo

Spanish Steps – Line A: Spagna

Appia Antica and Catacombs – Line A: Colli Albani and then bus 660

Taxis

Licenced taxis are white or yellow, have an identification number and are equipped with a meter which should be turned on at the start of the journey. You will find taxi-ranks dotted around the city. There are additional charges for a night service, luggage and airport shuttles. Beware of illegal taxi drivers (especially at the airport or train station), who will rip you off.

Car rental

Driving in Rome should be avoided if possible. The traffic is fast and furious, the one-way system is highly complex, there are long and frequent traffic jams, parking is difficult and car crime is rife. Several car hire firms have desks in Termini station, including Avis (*tel: (06) 4814373*), Hertz (*tel: (06) 4740389*) and Europcar (*tel: (06) 520811*).

Rome by scooter

When in Rome . . . do as the Romans and rent a Vespa from Bici and Baci (*Via del Viminale 5, tel: (06) 4828443*), I Bike Rome (*Via Veneto 156, tel: (06) 3225240*) or the Rent Scooter Center (*Via in Lucina 13/14, tel: (06) 6876455*). Make sure you have adequate insurance and read all the conditions of rental thoroughly.

Recommended city tours

On dry land

Several companies organise walking tours guided by archaeologists and art historians. Roman Walks (*tel: (06) 39728728*) operate in conjunction with Gruppo Archeologico Romano. Walks offered by Enjoy Rome (*tel: (06) 4451843*) include 'Ancient Rome', 'The Vatican City', a 'Night Tour' and a 3-hour leisurely guided bike-ride 'A Blast through the Past'.

ATAC Bus No. 110 offers a 2-hour tour of the city (without a guide), departing daily from Termini at 1400, 1500, 1700 and 1800. Otherwise several agencies provide guided tours in various languages. You will find leaflets with information and map routes at most tourist kiosks. Try Stop-'n'-Go's circular tours with 14 selected stops at key sights where you can hop on and off as you please. Ciao Roma's trolley tour is similar, but with 16 stops and individual audio guides in various languages.

On the water

The 'Tiber' boat departs from Ponte Umberto I (near Piazza Navona) daily (except Mondays, and during January and February) at 1030 and 1245 for a $1^1/_2$ hour tour to Ponte Duca d'Aosta and back. Contact Tourvisa (*Via Marghere 32, tel: (06) 4463481*) for information.

From the air

For the experience of a lifetime, and breathtaking aerial views of Rome and its environs, go on a hot-air balloon tour with Club Laziale Fiorenzo Mamertini (*tel: (06) 5298983*).

Don't miss

1 Campo de' Fiori

This relaxed and informal market in one of the city's most picturesque squares, with its down-to-earth barrow boys and cheerfully-striped awnings, offers a slice of real Roman life and all the tastes, fragrances and colours of Italian cuisine. A veritable feast for the senses! **Pages 58–73**

2 Colosseum

Once inside this 'must-see' monument that has so remarkably endured the test of time, it is easy to imagine the ecstatic crowds cheering the wild animals and the hapless gladiators fighting to the bitter, bloody end. **Pages 28–29**

3 Fontana di Trevi

Discovering the Trevi Fountain for the first time is one of Rome's most pleasant surprises – a monumental extravaganza of sea gods, horses and rock pools, squeezed into a tiny piazza amidst a maze of twisting lanes and alleyways. Before you leave, toss in a coin – an old custom which ensures that one day you will return! **Page 108**

4 Foro Romano

Walk the streets where Caesar once trod, the epicentre of an empire which embraced most of the known world and the very heart of ancient Rome. **Pages 31–35**

5 Musei Capitolini

The Capitoline Museums with their outstanding collection of Greek and Roman sculptures, provide an excellent overview of ancient art and history for first-time visitors to the city. **Pages 24–25**

6 Musei Vaticani and Cappella Sistina

The Vatican Museums count among the finest in the world, 7km of galleries and passageways culminating in Michelangelo's remarkably frescoed Sistine Chapel – probably the greatest artwork of all time. Pages 142–145

7 Pantheon

The Pantheon remains long in one's memory. Of all the city sights, its extraordinary near-perfect condition helps to bridge the two millennia in a way the many ruined buildings of ancient Rome cannot. Pages 80–81

19

8 Piazza Navona

More of a giant stage set of famous fountains and terracotta façades than a square, this is where Rome's heart beats the loudest, where the theatre of daily Roman life is re-enacted daily in one of Italy's greatest piazzas. Pages 50–51

9 San Pietro in Vaticano

Not only is St Peter's the largest church in Christendom and one of the world's most visited sights, but at sunset its massive dome is one of the most memorable silhouettes of the Roman skyline. Page 146

10 Scalinata di Trinità dei Monti

Sit awhile on the Spanish Steps at the heart of Rome's liveliest shopping district and watch the world go by. And on a blisteringly hot summer day, join tired shoppers cooling their feet in the well-placed fountain at their base! Page 97

Ancient
Rome

Here ancient Rome prospered, declined and fell. Given the presence of such mighty ruins as the Forum and the Colosseum, you might expect the neighbourhood to be fossilised by its very antiquity. Astonishingly, however, enough remains to enable visitors to imagine Imperial Rome in all its glory as the centre of religious, political and commercial life and the first city of a million inhabitants in Europe.

ANCIENT ROME

Ancient Rome

*Getting there: **By metro:** Metro B stops at the Colosseum (Colosseo). **By bus:** Buses to the Campidoglio include Nos. 44, 46, 56, 60, 715, 716 and 810. No. 95 also stops here from Via Veneto, as do No. 85 and 160 from Piazza San Silvestre. No. 64 stops in Piazza Venezia en route from the Vatican to Termini. For the Forum and Colosseum, take Nos. 87, 175, 186 and 850, which run the length of Via dei Fori Imperiali, or No.75 straight from Termini. Electric minibus No.117 also passes by the Colosseum. **By tram:** Tram No. 30 goes past the Colosseum.*

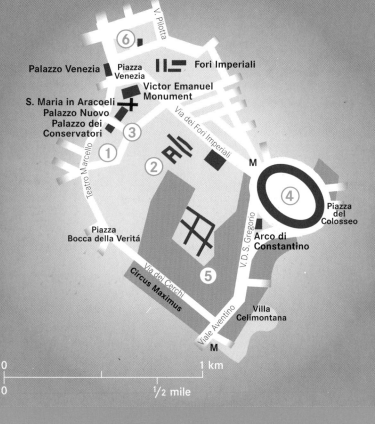

(1) Capitoline Hill

During the days of the Roman Empire, this – the smallest of Rome's Seven Hills – was the Capital of the Western world. It is also the site of the first modern piazza and the celebrated Capitoline Museums, crammed with treasures of antiquity, and therefore an ideal place to start a tour of Rome's ancient foundations. **Page 24**

(2) Roman Forum

The Forum was the heart of ancient Rome. Even if you're not an archaeology expert, it is worth spending some time here, sitting on a chunk of toppled marble surrounded by arches, pillars and porticoes, dreaming of the glories of empires past. **Pages 31–35**

(3) Admire the views

The Campidoglio presents the two faces of Rome. To the southeast (from the terrace behind Palazzo Senatorio) you can enjoy a breath-taking panorama of the Forum, along the Via Sacra to the Colosseum, while to the northwest (from the Cordonata stairway in Piazza del Campidoglio) the far-reaching vista of 'modern' Rome is best viewed at dusk. **Page 24**

(4) Colosseum

Built in 72 BC, the Colosseum is undoubtedly Rome's most stirring sight – the very symbol of its eternity. As the eighth-century English monk and historian, the Venerable Bede prophesied: 'While stands the Colosseum, Rome shall stand; When falls the Colosseum, Rome shall fall; And when Rome falls – the world.' **Pages 28–29**

(5) Palatine

According to legend, Romulus founded Rome here on the Palatine Hill. Today, it is the most romantic and relaxing of all the city's ancient sites; its ruins are shaded by fragrant pines, flecked with brilliantly-coloured flowers and cooled by a gentle sea breeze. The views from Palatine Hill are also sensational, overlooking both the Forum and the mighty Colosseum. **Pages 36–37**

(6) See the world's first comic strip

Trajan's Column, part of the Fori Imperiali, has been described as the world's first comic strip. The 210m of marble carvings spiralling up the column – considered the finest example of Roman sculpture – provide a vivid pictorial account of life in Roman times. **Page 30**

Tip

This district contains the majority of Rome's ancient remains, and traipsing around a load of ruins can be tedious if you are not well prepared. So remember to wear comfortable shoes and a sun hat, and to bring with you plenty to drink (to avoid the exorbitantly-priced refreshment stalls around here), a light pair of binoculars for the inaccessible details at the top of high arches and columns, a camera, plenty of film and, of course, your guidebook.

Tourist information

The tourist information booth is on Piazza del Tempio della Pace (Fori Imperiali). *Open daily 0900–1800 (tel: (06) 69924307).*

Campidoglio (Capitol)

Piazza del Campidoglio.

In ancient times, the Temple of Jupiter on the Capitol (the southern summit of Capitoline hill) marked the centre of the Roman Empire, the venue for all the most important religious and political ceremonies and the goal of every triumphal procession. Before long the hill came to symbolise Rome as *caput mundi*, capital of the world. Indeed, the concept of a 'capital' city comes from the Capitol.

Though the original temple and capitol buildings are long gone, Piazza del Campidoglio (*see page 26*) continues to play an historic role as the seat of the municipal government, and the site of the great Capitoline Museum, the oldest museum in Europe.

Musei Capitolini (Capitoline Museums)

Piazza del Campidoglio. Tel: (06) 67102071. Open Tue–Sat 0900–1900; Sun 0900–1330. Closed Mon. Admission: £££; free on the last Sun of the month. One ticket gains entrance to both palazzi.

The famous Capitoline Museums contain some of the finest and rarest treasures of ancient Rome, together with some major 16th- and 17th-century European paintings. These gorgeous collections are displayed inside two *palazzi* flanking Piazza del Campidoglio, designed by Michelangelo and lavishly decorated with gilt and coffered ceilings and frescoed walls.

On the north side, **Palazzo Nuovo** is devoted mainly to sculpture. Most of the finest pieces are Roman copies of Greek masterpieces, showing the fondness for Hellenistic art in ancient Rome – the poignant statue of the *Dying Gaul*, the athletic *Discobolus*, portraying the twisted

torso of a Greek discus thrower, a red porphyry marble *Drunken Faun* taken from Hadrian's Villa at Tivoli, and the voluptuous *Capitoline Venus*, walled up for centuries to avoid destruction by early Christians.

For those keen to put faces to the city's early rulers, or to the poets and thinkers of ancient Greece, the 'Hall of the Emperors' and the 'Hall of the Philosophers' contain characterful collections of busts. Look out also for the *Infant Hercules* wrestling with a snake, believed to be a portrait of Caracalla – the poor thing was already ugly at the age of 5; the marble *Portrait of a Flavian Lady*, with her elaborate mass of fanciful curls, a hairstyle all the rage among female aristocracy in 1 AD; and the bronze equestrian statue of debonair Marcus Aurelius (*see page 26*), the most recent addition to the palace.

On the opposite side of the square, the **Palazzo dei Conservatori** houses the rest of the Capitoline Museum. The courtyard is dominated by an amusing giant head, foot and pointing hand of Emperor Constantine – the remains of a colossal 10-metre-high seated statue from the Forum (*see page 35*). Inside, on the second floor, is a treasure trove of famous paintings including important canvases by Veronese, Tintoretto, Rubens, Titian, Caravaggio and others, while noteworthy sculptures on the ground floor include *Spinario*, a beautifully-poised bronze of a boy removing a thorn from his foot and *Esquiline Venus*, dating from the first century BC. The most celebrated piece is undoubtedly the *Capitoline She-Wolf*, an Etruscan bronze from the fifth century BC, which has become the symbol of Rome. The infants she is suckling were Renaissance additions, to illustrate one of the city's best-known legends – the story of Romulus and Remus.

Mythic origins

According to legend, Romulus and Remus were the founders of Rome. They were thrown into the Tiber by their uncle Amulus, the evil king of Alba, who had already ousted their father from the throne and saw them as potential claimants to his crown. However, they were washed ashore and suckled by a she-wolf until a kindly shepherd took them home. Subsequently, they founded a city on the site where they had been saved and called it 'Roma'.

Palazzo Venezia

Via del Plebiscito 118. Tel: (06) 6798865. Admission: ££.

Palazzo Venezia was one of the earliest Renaissance civic buildings in Rome, built in 1455 for the Venetian Cardinal Pietro Barbo, who later became Pope Paul II. Subsequently it became the Venetian Embassy, and more recently Benito Mussolini made it his headquarters, addressing his supporters from the tiny balcony overlooking the square. He used the *Sala del Mappamondo* (Map Room – named after its massive Renaissance painting of the world) for his office, delighting in its vast proportions, hoping to intimidate visitors with the long walk to his desk at the far end.

After the Allies liberated Rome in 1944, the palace was opened to the public for the first time. Today it houses one of the city's most underrated museums; its many precious tapestries, paintings, silver, ceramics, ancient arms and painted wood sculptures make it Rome's most important collection of decorative arts.

Piazza dei Campidoglio

Piazza dei Campidoglio.

It took 110 years to complete Rome's first modern piazza, a beautifully-cambered, trapezoid square designed so that the Capitoline Hill would turn its back on the Forum and pagan Rome to face St Peter's and the new Christian city. Following a commission from Pope Paul II to design a monumental complex worthy of the papal capital, Michelangelo rearranged the pre-existing buildings, constructed Palazzo Nuovo for symmetry, and designed the geometric paving and façades of all the palazzi surrounding the square. Finally, a gently rising, stately stone stairway was added called the *Cordonata*, leading out of Piazza Venezia, past larger-than-life Roman statues of Castor and Pollux, up to the elegant Capitol. The statue of Marcus Aurelius in the centre of the square is actually a modern copy of a second-century original – the oldest equestrian bronze to survive from antiquity – now in the Capitoline Museums.

> " *Rome is a continuity, called "eternal". What has accumulated in this place acts on everyone day and night, like an extra climate.* "
>
> **Elizabeth Bowen,**
> ***A Time in Rome*, 1960**

Santa Maria in Aracoeli
(St Mary of the Altar of Heaven)

Piazza d'Aracoeli. Open daily 0700–1200, 1600–1730 (1830 in summer).

Romans flock to this sixth-century church at the northern summit of the Capitoline, built on the site of the ancient Temple of Juno. They come to see its much-revered olive-wood Christ Child, said to be endowed with miraculous healing powers. Letters from all over the world addressed to *Il Bambino* surround the infant figure, and at Christmas it becomes the centrepiece of Rome's most famous crib scene. Other cherished treasures include the striking mosaic floor and Pinturicchio's great Renaissance frescoes telling *The Life of San Bernadino*.

The impressive Aracoeli Staircase – 124 steep, dazzling white marble steps built in 1348 in thanks for deliverance from the Black Death – offers a majestic approach to the church and wondrous views of the multi-domed skyscape of Rome.

Victor Emanuel Monument

Piazza Venezia.

Officially called Il Vittoriano, but perhaps more aptly nicknamed 'the wedding cake', 'the white typewriter' or 'Rome's false teeth', this massively bombastic, self-important white-marble edifice was built to celebrate the unification of Italy in 1870 and the country's first king, Victor Emanuel II. After World War I the Tomb of the Unknown Soldier was added at the top of the steps beneath a statue of the goddess Roma, and two 'eternal flames' were lit in the 1970s. It will never blend into the ochre tones of the surrounding buildings, but it does prove useful for orientation – an ugly white monster, easily spotted from high points throughout the city!

The Colosseum

The Colosseum must be seen to be believed! This stupendous four-tiered elliptical arena, built by Emperor Vespasian in AD 72, is the world's most famous amphitheatre and undoubtedly the most impressive of all the buildings of ancient Rome. Its statistics give an indication of its massive proportions: 57m high, built by 20,000 slaves and prisoners, with 80 arched entrances allowing easy access for over 55,000 spectators eager to watch the violent gladiatorial combats and other scenes of barbaric blood-letting. Emperor Titus opened the Colosseum in AD 80 with 100 days of games in which 9,000 animals were killed – leopards, lions, bears and a rhinoceros.

In its heyday, the entire building was encrusted with marble and ornamented by columns of Egyptian granite, fountains spurting perfumed water and stairways painted purple and gold. On hot days, a giant sailcloth awning called the *velarium* sheltered spectators from the elements. The audience would be seated according to social status with the front row seats in marble on the lowest tier for emperors, senators and civil servants, the second concrete tier for the bourgeoisie, the third for commoners. Women were confined to the uppermost reaches, except Vestal Virgins who sat near the emperor – an honour they did not always appreciate, frequently having to be escorted to the aptly-named *vomitorium* backstage.

Blood sports

The games were part of daily life in Rome, with the arena packed from dawn to dusk with spectators eagerly watching the violent gladiatorial combats and other such scenes of barbaric blood-letting (*see pages 40–41*). The most popular (and bloodiest!) 'spectator sports' were when wild animals, starved in advance, devoured defenceless condemned criminals. From the higher tiers, you can see a maze of dungeons and passages beneath the caved-in floor of the arena, where wild animals were kept in cages then winched to arena level. If a cowardly gladiator ever tried to retreat into the underground chambers, he was pushed out again with whips and red-hot irons to fight until death.

Chequered history

With the fall of the Empire, the Colosseum fell into disuse. In the Middle Ages it became the fortress of the Frangipani family. During the Renaissance the ruins were plundered

and stripped of their precious marble, travertine and metal to create palaces and churches throughout the city. In 1744, Pope Benedict XIV halted the quarrying and consecrated the arena to the Christian martyrs who died there. More recently, in the Fascist era, Mussolini was drawn by the power which the Colosseum represented, and demolished over 5,000 Medieval and Renaissance buildings (the length of Via dei Fori Imperiali) to create a clear view of it from his balcony at Palazzo Venezia. Today, thousands of tourists crowd into the Colosseum daily to marvel at this 'eighth wonder of the world' – as Lord Byron described it 'the gladiator's bloody circus … a noble wreck in ruinous perfection'.

Getting there: Piazza del Colosseo. Tel: (06) 7004261. Open daily 0900–dusk. Admission: £££.

66 *I really did not gain a suggestion of the astonishing size of it [the Colosseum] until I entered through one of the many arches … It was impossible not to be impressed by the thought of the emperors sitting on their especial balcony; the thousands upon thousands of Romans intent upon some gladiatorial feat.* 99

Theodore Dreiser, *A Traveller at Forty*, 1914

Fori Imperiali
(The Imperial Forums)

Via dei Fori Imperiali.

The Imperial Forums were built as an extension to the Roman Forum, as Rome grew into a burgeoning Empire – a series of five forums named after the rulers of the day: Augustus, Caesar, Vespasian, Nerva and Trajan. Some of the remains lie partially buried and unexcavated beneath Via dei Fori Imperiali – paved over by Mussolini to create a massive avenue for his military parades. Of the visible remains, the **Foro di Traiano (Trajan's Forum)** is the biggest, covering an area greater than four football pitches.

The greatest treasure of the Imperial Forums is **Colonna Traiana (Trajan's Column)** – a pristine white marble column 40m high, once topped with a bronze statue of Trajan, but since replaced by one of St Peter. It is decorated with some 26,000 carved figures that spiral up the column, chronicling Trajan's military victories in Dacia (now Romania) and providing a remarkable pictorial account of life and warfare in Roman times. Like many important monuments, the figures would originally have been painted in bright colours. The Greek and Latin libraries of the Forum would have stood close enough to the column for the artwork on its upper reaches to be viewed from their roof gardens.

Nearby, a six-storey, semicircular shopping mall – the **Mercati di Traiano (Trajan's Markets)** – provides a further fascinating insight into Roman life. It once boasted over 150 shops, selling fruit and flowers on the ground floor, oil and wine on the next, pepper, spices and other exotic goods on the third and fourth floors, with offices on the fifth and fishponds on the sixth. *Entrance on via IV Novembre 94. Tel: (06) 6790048. Open Tue–Sat 0900–1800; Sun 0900–1300. Closed Mon. Admission: ££.*

Foro Romano I
(The Roman Forum)

Via dei Fori Imperiali (to the north) and Via San Gregorio (to the east).
Tel: (06) 6780782. Open Mon–Sat 0900–1800 (1500 in winter); Sundays
0900–1300. Closed 1 Jan, 1 May, 25 Dec. Admission: £. Portable sound-guides
(££) are available for hire at the Via dei Fori Imperiali entrance (bring some
form of ID as a deposit).

The expression 'All roads lead to Rome' dates back to ancient times, when all roads led to the Forum – a magnificent cluster of temples, arches, memorials and halls of dazzling white marble with gleaming golden roofs that formed the heart of the ancient city. Once simply a narrow strip of marshy land between the Palatine and Capitoline hills, this is where Republican Rome began; where Cicero stirred the masses with his rousing orations; where Mark Antony came 'to bury Caesar, not to praise him'; where the sacred fire of the Eternal City was maintained and where victorious emperors showed off their spoils from the battles that made Rome *caput mundi*, capital of the world.

The forum was the centre of political, commercial and judicial life, as well as a community centre where people strolled under the porticoes and attended sports events. Over the centuries it was embellished with splendid temples and basilicas built by successive emperors, each seeking to outdo their predecessors and to immortalise themselves in stone.

Since the fall of Rome, the Forum has survived fire and earthquakes, barbarian invasions, grazing cows and Renaissance marble diggers. Its temples have been transformed into churches, its toppled pillars and venerable colonnades lost under layers of time. Serious excavation of the site only really began in 1898 and still continues today.

" Veni, vidi, vinci.
(I came, I saw,
I conquered) "

Julius Caesar

Foro Romano II
(The Roman Forum, continued)

Miraculously, enough remains of the Forum to evoke the past and to provide a unique walk through ancient Rome. The best way to make sense of the Forum is to enter the complex on Via dei Fori Imperiali and to start in the right-hand corner near the main road. Here you will find the Curia (Senate House), the very first assembly hall of the Roman elders, begun by Caesar in 44 BC, dedicated by Augustus in 29 BC and rebuilt by Diocletian in AD 203. This was the political heart of the Republic, where the senate discussed matters of the day in their fine white togas. Meetings were always conducted with the doors open so that public could be kept informed. The Curia was converted into a Christian Church in AD 203, but the current building (a replica of Diocletian's, with the original red and green marble floor) dates from 1937.

In front of the Curia, The Lapis Niger (Black Stone), protected by a concrete shelter, is one of the most sacred objects of the Forum. It supposedly marks the tomb of Romulus, the mythical founder of the city. Behind, the grandiose triple-arched Arco di Settimio Severo (Arch of Septimius Severus) dominates the western end of the Forum. The fine carvings on the arch originally commemorated the victories of the emperor and his two sons, Geta and Caracalla. However, at a later date, Caracalla had his brother murdered in the arms of their mother and then deleted all references to Geta from public monuments, replacing them with laudatory inscriptions to himself – hence the coarse chisel marks on some of the reliefs.

Beside the arch a piece of stone, once part of a third-century circular temple called the **Umbilicus Urbis**, marked the symbolic centre of Rome. Nearby stood the **Milarium Aureum (Golden Milestone)**. All roads led to Rome … to this very spot where a marble column recorded in gilded bronze letters the distances to all the major cities of the new Empire.

To the left lie the semicircular steps of the **Rostra**, a public platform for important speeches and ceremonies, named after the bronze prows (*rostra*) taken from defeated enemy ships in the Battle of Antium (338 BC), which once adorned it. The surrounding area was decorated with the three plants considered essential for Mediterranean prosperity – vines, olives and figs – which have since been replanted here. The eight tall columns beyond the Rostra once formed the entrance to the **Tempio di Saturno (Temple of Saturn)**. Built in 497 BC, it was one of the earliest temples in Rome and scene of the merry December Saturnalia festivities – the pagan precursor of Christmas – when masters and slaves were briefly equal and gifts were exchanged. The temple marks the start of the **Via Sacra (Sacred Way)**, the most famous street in ancient Rome, along which victorious generals in grand four-horse chariots rode the length of the Forum in triumphal procession to the Capitoline Hill to give thanks to Jupiter.

🔖 *The Via Sacra*

" *At each step, a palace, a ruin, a garden, a desert, a little house, a stable, a triumphal arch, a colonnade, and all these so close together that one could draw them on a small sheet of paper.* **"**

J W Von Goethe, *The Italian Journey*, 1786–8

Foro Romano III
(The Roman Forum, continued)

Heading eastwards, the Via Sacra runs alongside the sparse remains of Caesar's huge **Basilica Giulia,** *which set the trend for enormous buildings in the Forum, used as a courthouse and meeting place of the four civic tribunals. It seems they did not work very hard … look closely and you will see board games carved into some of its surviving steps!*

The next recognisable monument on your right is the **Tempio di Castore e Polluce (Temple of Castor and Pollux)**, with three Corinthian columns topped with a frieze from the time of Augustus. It was dedicated to the two mysterious horsemen who led the Romans to victory over the Etruscans in 499 BC, whose identity was later revealed as that of the 'Heavenly Twins'.

Heading towards the Via dei Fori Imperiali entrance, little is left of the **Tempio di Cesare (Temple of Caesar)**, the building which began the cult of Emperor worship. Following his death (*see page 67*), on the Ides of March in 44 BC, Caesar's body was cremated here. The people grieved so much that they kept his funeral pyre burning for days, washed his ashes with milk and wine, buried them and built a temple on the site.

By contrast the **Tempio di Antonio e Faustina (Temple of Antoninus and Faustina)**, built in AD 2, is the only Forum building remaining that indicates the monumental size of these ancient temples. The original six columns and porch, decorated with a beautiful frieze of griffins and candelabra, were saved from destruction by the temple's re-consecration as the Renaissance **Church of San Lorenzo in Miranda.**

Opposite, the circular, white marble **Tempio di Vesta (Temple of Vesta)** contained the sacred fire that symbolised Rome's eternity. It was kept alight by Vestal Virgins, the only female priesthood in Rome, who entered divine service as young girls and lived a chaste life in the neighbouring **Atrium Vestae (House of the Vestal Virgins)**, today striking for its graceful statues, rose garden and pond.

Continuing along the Via Sacra, you will pass the tiny round **Tempio di Romolo (Temple of Romulus)**, incorporated into the sixth-century Franciscan Church of Saints Cosmas and Damian, known for its early mosaics and frescoes. Beyond it lie the scattered remains of the **Basilica di Costantino e Massenzio (Basilica of Constantine and Maxentius)**, one of the last great constructions of Imperial Rome, containing Constantine's colossal statue of himself (*see page 25*). During the Renaissance, the basilica was used by Michelangelo and Bramante as the model for St Peter's Basilica.

Next door, the tenth-century church of **Santa Francesca Romana** incorporates part of the **Tempio di Venere e Roma (Temple of Venus and Roma)**. Once the largest temple in Rome, it was partly bulldozed by Mussolini to make way for his grand military boulevard. Today St Frances has the unfortunate task of being Rome's patron saint of automobile drivers. Every year, thousands of taxi drivers attend their annual blessing here.

" The Forum, grey and desolate, in its ruined state. Only dust. Not a patch of grass, only a few blades sprouting between the paving stones of the Via Sacra. "

Emile Zola

Marking the eastern end of the Forum, the **Arco di Tito (Arch of Titus)** is the oldest triumphal arch in Rome, built by Domitian to celebrate the victories of his brother Titus. The beautifully-preserved reliefs show on one side Titus returning from battle in a chariot and, on the other, the triumphal procession displaying his war spoils from Jerusalem.

The Palatine

Of Rome's seven hills, it is the Palatine – the city's legendary birthplace, with its most romantic garden – which always captures the visitor's imagination. What's more, its lush vegetation makes it a peaceful, cool and shady retreat in which to relax for a few hours far away from the noisy, frenetic city centre. The first of Rome's seven hills to be inhabited, this is where Romulus allegedly founded the city (see page 25) and you can see traces of huts from as early as 800 BC.

A desirable residence

For centuries, Palatino was a highly sought-after address. In Republican times, the Roman nobility lived on the hill, including Cicero, Octavian and Agrippa. When Octavian became the Emperor Augustus, the Palatine began to alter. He had a series of fine houses built for himself and his wife Livia including **Casa di Livia (Livia's House)**, whose small rooms still contain remnants of mosaic floors, wall paintings and lead drainage piping engraved with *IVLIAE AV* (Julia Augusta).

All the emperors after Augustus lived here, each adding his own new palace. With Augustus' successor Tiberius commissioning the great **Domus Tiberiana**, then Domitian constructing the massive **Domus Augustana (House of the August one)**, the entire Palatine soon became covered in the grand residences, and the words 'palatial' and 'palace' were coined. Nero even built a **Cryptoporticus** – a network of underground tunnels 140m long – linking all the palaces. Legend has it that Caligula was stabbed in the tunnel. Near Domus Augustana, the **Antiquarium** museum contains a variety of antique Palatino treasures, although the more valuable pieces have been removed to the National Roman Museum (*see page 110*). Sadly little remains of the **Domus**

Flavia, at one time the hub of imperial activity on the hill. This vast complex once contained a basilica, banqueting hall, *nyphaeum* (where diners retired for breaks between courses), baths, porticoes, throne room and a fountain in the form of a maze. Emperor Domitian is said to have lined the throne room with mirrors so that he could see approaching enemies from any angle.

🔖 *Domus Flavia*

Septimius Severus, the last emperor to build on the Palatine, positioned his palatial seven-storey **Domus Severiana** on the southeastern tip of the hill in order to impress visitors arriving in Rome. Today, only the massive arcaded foundations remain, overlooking the **Circus Maximus** below the Palatine, the biggest horse-and-chariot racecourse throughout the Roman Empire, capable of seating 2,000 spectators on tiers of marble seats in its heyday.

The world's first botanical garden

Following the fall of Rome, even the early kings of Rome chose to live in the remodelled imperial palaces here, as did the first popes. In medieval times, the Palatine became an important ecclesiastical centre, with monasteries filling some of the buildings. In the Renaissance, two wealthy families, the Barbarini and the Farnese, sealed the hill's illustrious reputation by building summer houses here. The Farnese also filled in the Domus Tiberiana and planted the **Orti Farnesiani (Farnese Gardens)**, the world's first botanical garden. From its terraces, the views over the Forum and the city beyond are unsurpassed.

Getting there: Via dei Fori Imperiali (on the north) and Via San Gregorio (on the east). Tel: (06) 6780782. Open Mon–Sat 0900–1800 (1500 in winter); Sunday 0900–1300. Closed 1 Jan, 1 May, 25 Dec. Admission: £££.

" *Cypress and ivy, weed and wallflower grown*
Matted and mass'd together, hillocks heap'd
On what were chambers, arch crush'd, column strown
In fragments, choked up vaults, and frescos steep'd
In subterranean damps … "

Lord Byron

Cafés and bars

Caffè della Studente
Via delle Terme di Tito 94. No tel. £. Closed Sun. This popular student hangout offers excellent value sandwiches, pizza slices, cheeseburgers, beers and coffee to eat on a sunny pavement terrace or to take away.

Cavour 313
Via Cavour 313. Tel: (06) 6785496. ££. Closed Sun. One of Rome's best-loved *enotece* (wine bars). Wash down typical Roman pub grub – savoury pies, *torta rustica* (quiche), pasta, patés, sausage and cheese platters – with wines of the region.

Gelateria La Dolce Vita
Via Cavour 306. No tel. £. Treat the kids to an ice-cream or a frozen yoghurt here, after a visit to the Forum.

Mille Panini
Via Eudossiana 20. Tel: (06) 486671. £. Closed Sun. Feeling peckish? Then come to this take-away bar for a choice of over 35 tasty sandwiches, followed by a slice of banana, nutella and mascarpone pizza for dessert!

San Clemente
Via S Giovanni in Laterano 124. Tel: (06) 70450944. £. Closed Sun. Typically Italian spit'n'sawdust stand-up bar, with sandwiches, *tavola calda* (hot snacks), coffee, ice creams and a tiny pavement terrace opposite the celebrated church of San Clemente.

Tip

As this area is one of the main tourist honey-pots, restaurants tend to be of poor quality and often a complete rip-off. Steer clear of sandwich stands, and either bring a picnic to enjoy atop Palatine Hill or in Parco di Traiano or take time to explore the side-streets of the neighbourhood, where your efforts will be richly rewarded.

Nightlife

*You won't find much nightlife around here except at **Folkstudio** (Via Frangipane 42, tel: (06) 4871063, closed Mon), a tiny venue staging live experimental music nightly. There's no bar though so bring your own drinks! For classical entertainment, ask the tourist office for details of any open-air summer concerts in Piazza dei Campidoglio.*

Shopping

*Apart from a small morning fruit and vegetable market in Via SS Quattro (*open daily except Sun*) and La Voglia, a delightful delicatessen at 295 Via Cavour, concentrate your shopping efforts on the area around Piazza Venezia and Via del Corso (*see page 87*), where you will find Real for menswear, Stefanel and Pazza Venezia for ladies fashions, Punto Zero for shoes and bags and one of the city's largest Benetton stores.*

Restaurants

Ai Tre Scalini
Via SS Quattro 30. Tel: (06) 7096309. £££. Closed Mon. Reservations essential. One of the best restaurants in Rome, small and unpretentious, with inventive Roman cuisine, just two blocks east of the Colosseum.

Mario's
Piazza del Grillo 9. Tel: (06) 6793725. ££. Closed Sun. Hidden up the hill behind the Imperial Fora, this intimate restaurant serves such traditional local dishes as *spaghetti alla carbonara*, *saltimbocca* and *trippa alla romana* on a small, leafy terrace.

Nerone
Via delle Terme di Tito 96. Tel: (06) 4745207. ££. Closed Sun and August. Reservation recommended. A Roman institution serving generous portions of hearty country-style cuisine. Try the *rigatoni* with potatoes, followed by roasted spring lamb.

Taverna Ulpia
Foro Traiano 1b/2. Tel: (06) 6789980. ££. Closed Sun. Classified as an historical monument, Rome's oldest restaurant looks out over Trajan's Forum. It's a shame that the food is not as good as the view.

Valentino
Via Cavour 293. Tel: (06) 4881303. ££. Closed Fri. Reservation recommended. This tiny trattoria serves an excellent value menu turistico together with traditional Roman cuisine – *gnocchi* on Thursdays, tripe on Saturdays. Ideal for lunch.

Roman entertainment

*The emperors continually sought to make themselves popular with the masses by building public baths, theatres and amphitheatres in which to stage games. The theatre never really caught on, nor did 'Greek-style' athletics competitions such as those held in the **Circus Agonalis** (Piazza Navona, see pages 50–51) with prizes for athletic prowess and artistic achievement.*

The crowds much preferred the thrills of the Colosseum – live killing matches between pairs of gladiators, butchering one another to the cries of 'Jugula!' (Slit his throat!). They all loved the crowd participation – a wounded gladiator could beg for mercy by raising his left hand; if they waved handkerchiefs he was saved. More often than not, however, he would get the 'thumbs down' sign, meaning death.

'Ave Caesar! Morituri te Salutant!'

Human sacrifice as a sport was introduced during the First Punic War to make the Romans better soldiers –

indifferent to the sight of death, blood and gore. Day-long spectacles would start with the grand arrival of the Emperor and his cortège, followed by a trumpet fanfare and a procession of gladiators – mostly slaves, prisoners of war or condemned criminals but sometimes volunteers too – pathetically chanting *'Hail Caesar! Those about to die salute you!'*. Animals, performing tricks rather like modern circus acts, would then be followed by such cruel spectacles as the bloody fights between two wild beasts or between man and a pre-starved lion, tiger or bear. Each time someone was killed, attendants dressed as Charon (the mythical ferryman of the dead) would carry his body off and rake sand over the blood ready for the next bout.

The bloodier the better

Another hugely popular 'sport' were the contests between gladiator 'duellers'; convicted criminals – one armed, one not – the first obliged to kill the second. The 'victor' was then disarmed and exposed to an armed rival and so on until a single gladiator remained, who had his throat slit. At one such spectacle celebrating the 1,000th anniversary of the founding of Rome, over 2,000 gladiators took part, and 60 lions, 32 elephants, 12 tigers and 10 giraffes were slaughtered.

Gladiator duels were eventually banned in AD 404 by Emperor Honorius and wild animal fights disappeared in the sixth century.

Around Piazza Navona

For centuries this bustling area has been the true heart of Rome – the centro storico *or 'historic centre'. Anchored by the majestic Piazza Navona, one of the most animated squares in Rome, its tightly-knit tangle of crumbling medieval lanes and picturesque fountain-filled piazzettas offers excellent restaurants, superb shopping, and a host of ancient churches brimming with treasures of the Baroque.*

AROUND PIAZZA NAVONA

Getting there: **By bus:** *Take Nos. 46, 62 or 64 which pass to the south of Piazza Navona along Corso Vittorio Emanuele II, or Nos. 70, 81, 87, 492 or 628 which pass to the east along Corso del Rinascimento, while No. 280 follows the course of the river around the northern perimeter of the district.*

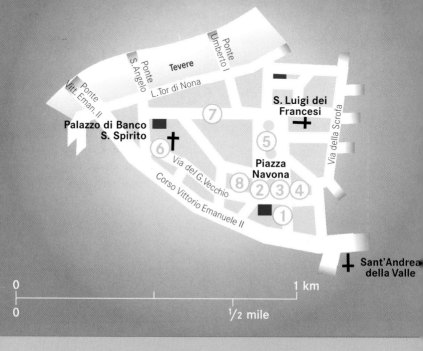

AROUND PIAZZA NAVONA

① Museo di Roma

Make this museum your first port of call. Once you have a grasp of Rome's colourful history since the Middle Ages you will find subsequent walks in the *centro storico* all the more rewarding. **Page 48**

② Piazza Navona

Piazza Navona is one of Italy's most impressive piazzas. After strolling through the labyrinth of surrounding streets, it is exhilarating to enter its vast open space (best approached for the first time from the east or south) and to sit day or night on a café terrace or beside one of its famous fountains, soaking up the sun and the atmosphere. **Pages 50–51**

③ Try Tartufo

They say you haven't experienced Rome until you've tasted the *tartufo* – an extravagant double dose of rich chocolate ice cream – at Tre Scalini. Savour it whilst taking in the sights of Piazza Navona. **Page 54**

④ An entertaining souvenir

Have your portrait sketched in just five minutes by one of the many street artists of Piazza Navona or, if you want a good laugh, by a caricaturist.

⑤ Fontana dei Quattro Fiumi

The 'Fountain of the Four Rivers' is undoubtedly one of Rome's finest fountains. In true Bernini style, its elegance and majesty transcends the bombast of the Baroque. Even the water is used as a sculptural element.
Page 47

⑥ Go to church

Rome is widely considered the city where Baroque architecture found its strongest and most individual expression. Here in the *centro storico* you will be dazzled by the multitude of resplendent Baroque churches. **Pages 46 and 52–53**

⑦ Shop for antiques

This historic district is the centre of Rome's antiques trade. The shops along Via dei Coronari, housed in fine Renaissance *palazzi*, sell everything from ancient Roman busts to Baroque cherubs. **Page 55**

⑧ Voice your opinion

Pin your comments about the city on the crumbling statue of Pasquino, the chattiest of Rome's 'talking statues'. But be careful what you say… in the olden days, the penalty for leaving messages here was death! **Page 49**

45

Tip

For that special occasion, the tempting candle-lit restaurants, atmospheric cafés and wine bars spilling out onto Piazza Navona are hard to beat. Such a superb setting does not come cheaply, but just a stone's throw from the square, the narrow maze of streets conceals a host of cheerful, less touristic and better-value eateries.

Tourist information

The tourist information booth is at Piazza delle Cinque Lune, just north of Piazza Navona. *Open daily 0900–1800 (tel: (06) 68809240).*

Chiesa Nuova and Oratorio de Filippini

Piazza della Chiesa Nuova, Corso Vittorio Emanuele. Open daily 0800–1200, 1630–1900. Admission: £ (admission to the Oratorio is available only on request to the caretaker).

This spacious 'New Church' was the seat of San Filippo Neri's Oratorians, one of the most important movements of the Counter-Reformation in the late 16th century. It was built on the site of a smaller church called Santa Maria in Valicella, to enable Neri to preach Catholicism to the masses as a defence against sweeping Protestantism.

On entering the church, it is hard to believe the interior was once simple, white-washed and spartan, in keeping with Neri's precepts. Half a century after his death, ecclesiastical fashions changed and the then fashionable Baroque artist **Pietro da Cortona** smothered the apse, cupola and nave with exuberant frescos, setting the trend for all the other churches in 17th-century Rome. **Caravaggio** produced a *Descent from the Cross* (later moved to the Vatican and replaced by a copy in the second chapel on the right), **Barocci** provided *The Visitation* (fourth chapel on the left) and *The Presentation in the Temple* (in the left transept), and the choir was decorated with three masterpieces by the young Rubens.

Next door, the **Oratorio**, with its innovative rippling brick façade by Borromini, was built between 1637 and 1662 as the centre of Neri's religious order. Here his followers (called *Filippini*) gathered to meditate and listen to sacred music, thereby creating a new musical genre – the *oratorio*.

Words of wisdom

Outside the Chiesa Nuova, a fountain (called the **Fontana della Terrina** *because it resembles a soup tureen) bears the inscription:*

Ama Dio e non falire – fa del bene e lascia dire

('Love God and don't fail – do good and make sure people talk about it')

Fontana dei Quattro Fiumi
(Fountain of the Four Rivers)

Piazza Navona.

The magnificent centrepiece of Piazza Navona – a dynamic *tour de force* of marble and rushing water created by Gianlorenzo Bernini – is one of the great treasures of Baroque art in Rome, and a symbol of the city. It was commissioned in 1651 by Pope Innocent X, who incurred the wrath of the Roman population by taxing bread in order to finance the project. His reputation never recovered, but the end result turned out to be a brilliant investment of public funds.

The imposing fountain symbolises the four corners of the world, enlightened and dominated by the Pope. The four powerful allegorical statues, sitting atop a rocky grotto adorned with tropical plants, shells, a lion and a sea monster, represent the **rivers Danube**, **Nile**, **Ganges** and **Plate**. The entire ensemble is crowned with an ancient Egyptian obelisk (taken from the circus of Maxentius on the Via Appia Antica, *see pages 160–161*) and the family crest of Pope Innocent X – a dove holding an olive branch.

Stories about the fountain abound … Apparently Bernini stole the commission for the fountain from his arch-rival Borromini by bribing the Pope's lady-friend, Olympic Maidalchini, with a solid silver model of his design. It is often said that the Nile is covering his face in horror at the sight of Borromini's church façade behind the fountain (Sant' Agnese, *see page 51*) and that Plate has his hand raised in fear lest the church should collapse. In fact, the face of the Nile is covered as its source was then unknown. Borromini did not even start work on the church until after the fountain was completed.

Museo di Roma (Palazzo Braschi)

Piazza San Pantaleo 10. Tel: (06) 6875880.

Don't be put off by the sober exterior of this vast, triangular-shaped building as the stern, heavy façade belies a lavishly decorated interior and a fascinating museum – the Museum of Rome – devoted to the history of the city from the Middle Ages to the last century.

The most rewarding part of the museum is a display of paintings and drawings that vividly evoke the life of medieval Rome. They include theatrical paintings of jousting and carriages in the flooded Piazza Navona, showy scenes of papal entertainment through the centuries and a stunning series of city views by Ippolito Caffi. However, pride of place goes to Pope Pius IX's personal railway carriage (1857), used for journeys between Rome and Frascati.

Palazzo Braschi also has a unique past. Built in the late 18th century, it was the last of the Roman palaces to be constructed for a pope's family. Following a brief spell as the Ministry of the Interior in the late 19th century, the fascist Federation of Rome took it over in 1930, and it eventually became a municipal museum in 1952.

Currently closed for restoration, the museum is provisionally scheduled for reopening in November 1999.

Palazzo del Banco di Santo Spirito

Via del Banco di Santo Spirito. Open normal banking hours. Admission: £.

Just off the heavily trafficked Corso Vittorio Emanuale, this hidden gem was once the Mint of papal Rome and is still often called the Antica Zecca (Old Mint). The upper storeys of the early 16th-century façade are in the shape of a Roman triumphal arch, with two Baroque statues symbolising Thrift and Charity looking down on passers-by from the roof. Above the doorway an inscription records the founding of the Banco di Santo Spirito (today part of the Banco di Roma) by Pope Paul V in 1605 to service the financial needs of visiting pilgrims and churchmen to the nearby Vatican (*see pages 136–153*).

Pasquino

Piazza di Pasquino

" What the Barbarians didn't do, the Barberini did. "

One of Pasquino's witty anti-establishment remarks

Pasquino – the rather forlorn third-century BC sculpture with a limbless, twisted torso and weather-beaten face, propped against the wall of Palazzo Braschi – is the most loquacious of all Rome's 'talking statues'. Originally one of a group of Homeric heroes decorating Domitian's circus (*see page 50*), it was placed here in 1501 near the shop of local Vatican tailor and gossip-monger Pasquino who, much to the amusement

of his customers, would attach to it witty comments on current events. Freedom of speech was not encouraged under papal rule so, in a city hardly renowned for its tolerance, discontented citizens would creep into the square at dead of night to attach libellous anti-establishment complaints, satires and pamphlets to the statue, making 'Pasquino' a Renaissance equivalent of *Private Eye*.

49

'Pasquino' soon gained correspondents as his scandalous verses were 'answered' by other talking statues, including Madame Lucrezia (on Piazza Venezia), Mariforio (in the courtyard of Palazzo Nuovo), Luigi Abate (beside Sant-Andrea della Valle) and Il Facchino, the talking fountain (*see pages 78–79*). By the 18th century, these 'written crimes' were severely punishable by law. One of Pope Benedict XIII's decrees threatened 'the death penalty, the confiscation of assets and the vilification of the name … of any one who writes, prints or distributes libels of the kind known as pasquinades', although there is no record of the death penalty ever being carried out.

Even today, Pasquino is used by people with political or social axes to grind, and those wishing to make a jibe at local issues. With Rome's ever-changing government there is rarely a shortage of material!

Piazza Navona

No visitor to Rome should miss Piazza Navona. For centuries this atmospheric pedestrian square has been one of the main hubs of Roman social life. It occupies the site of an ancient sports stadium, the Circus of Domitian of AD 86, hence its unusually long, thin shape. Hidden beneath the foundations of the surrounding buildings is the arena's original seating for 30,000 spectators and most streets leading into the piazza were once entrances into the stadium. Via Agonale recalls the athletes who entered here for the races. The stadium was known as the Circus Agonalis (arena for athletes), corrupted to n'Agone and eventually Navona.

During the Middle Ages, the 'arena for athletes' was occupied by vineyards, but with Rome's rebirth in the 15th century it became an important marketplace, and continued thus for many centuries. Piazza Navona has provided the backdrop for countless processions, jousting competitions and other sporting spectacles including mock naval battles or *naumachiae*. The surface of the piazza was concave, and could be flooded by blocking the fountains' drains. As recently as the last century, it was annually flooded in the coldest winters for skating and at weekends during the stifling heat of summer, so cardinals and princes could cool off as their gilded carriages were driven around the water-filled piazza.

Papal spending spree

It was in the 17th century that Piazza Navona was transformed into the glorious Baroque square we see today, when Pamphili Pope Innocent X decided to embellish it in honour of his family. He commissioned the monumental **Fontana dei Quattro Fiumi** (*see page 47*) in the centre and ordered the restoration of the two 16th-century fountains – **Fontana del Moro** to the south, portraying a Moor hunting a dolphin by Bernini (the original sculptures are in the Villa Borghese Gardens, *see page 162*) and Fontana del Nettuno to the north, showing Neptune struggling with a sea-monster. Finally, he built his dream house – the **Palazzo Pamphili** – in the southwest corner of the square. Its gallery was decorated in 1650 by Pietro da Cortona with a vast fresco of the Aeneid, which runs the entire length of the building, today home to the Brazilian embassy.

Innocent then added a family chapel dedicated to **Sant' Agnese**, at the site where the pious 13-year-old virgin had supposedly been flung naked into a brothel in AD 304 in punishment for refusing to marry, but was saved from shame by the sudden and miraculous growth of long tresses – a scene portrayed in marble relief on the altar. The church was designed as one of the showpieces of the Baroque by Borromini. His characteristically convex façade perfectly balances the dome and towers and the dazzling interior also brims with architectural artifice, making the round dome seem elliptical and the shallow apses appear equal to the longer ones.

Still a circus

Today, life in the piazza revolves around its many pricey open-air cafés. The amazing collection of buildings coloured in every shade of ochre provides the perfect backdrop for people-watching from early morning through to the small hours – businessmen on mobile phones, tourists marvelling at the sights, locals chatting on marble benches, grandmothers strolling with grandchildren, nuns, artists, artisans, buskers, caricaturists, fortune-tellers, and couples entwined in passionate embrace. The Piazza has always been a circus – and always will be!

Befana

Piazza Navona is at its most colourful at the Christmas Befana market, named after the witch who gives children presents or coal depending on their behaviour. The square comes alive with sparkling stalls of toys, tinsel, cribs and even 'coal' sweets. A real treat … especially for children!

San Luigi dei Francesi

Piazza San Luigi dei Francesi. Open daily (except Thur pm) 0800–1230, 1530–1900. Admission: £.

The *pièce de resistance* of the French national church in Rome is undoubtedly Caravaggio's 'St Matthew' cycle (1599–1602), a trio of paintings hidden in the gloomy fifth chapel on the left near the main altar. Put some coins in the light machine and *The Calling of St Matthew*, *The Martyrdom of St Matthew* and *St Matthew and the Angel* will be miraculously revealed. These three great masterworks demonstrate the artist's characteristic use of light – casting the backgrounds into deep darkness to focus attention on the powerful imagery – and his typically realistic figures. This down-to-earth, everyday quality was considered irreverent at the time, and *St Matthew and the Angel* (above the altar) was initially rejected by the church. Never before had a saint been portrayed as an exhausted old man with dirty feet!

Sant' Andrea della Valle

Piazza Sant' Andrea della Valle, Corso Vittorio Emanuele. Open daily 0730–1200, 1630–1930. Admission: £.

This vast Baroque church boasts two main claims to fame: it has Rome's second highest dome after St Peter's (built by Carlo Maderno in 1625), but it is also famous as the setting for Act One of Puccini's *Tosca*, the only opera set in a church. Today's setting is somewhat less romantic . . . on one of Rome's busiest thoroughfares. Hard to imagine that, in Roman times, the *valles* (valley) was the site of a large lake.

" *Now I have arrived, I have calmed down and feel as if I had found peace that will last for my whole life.* "

J W von Goethe, *The Italian Journey*, 1786–8

Inside 'Sant' Andrea of the Valley', you will be struck by the flamboyant, gilded interior, smothered in frescoes by Lanfranco and rival painter, Domenichino. Lanfranco nearly died while painting the extravagant *Glory of Paradise* in the dome, supposedly because the jealous Domenichino sabotaged the scaffolding on which he was working. Domenichino, in a later attempt to upstage him, produced such radical frescoes in the four pendentives of the dome that even in later years, French novelist and consul Stendhal was led to remark: 'There are days when it seems to me painting can go no further'.

On leaving the church, look closely at the almost perfectly balanced, symmetrical façade and you will spot one obvious flaw. Rainaldi, the designer, decided to use sculpted angels rather than traditional scrolls at the corners to fuse the upper and lower halves of the building. He commissioned Cosimo Fancelli to make two angels but, on hearing that the first angel had been criticised by Pope Alexander VII, Fancelli declared: 'If the Pope wants another angel, he'll have to make it himself!' To this day, there remains only one angel.

Via dei Coronari

Via dei Coronari, one of the city's most famous shopping streets, has been making a living out of tourists ever since the 15th century, when it started out as the Via Recta (Straight Street), leading directly to the Vatican. Within a few years, rosary makers (*coronari*) had taken over the street, doing a roaring trade selling their religious mementos to the constant throng of pilgrims approaching St Peter's. Nowadays, its majestic Renaissance *palazzi* contain fine antiques shops (*see page 55*) and upmarket art

galleries and twice a year, in the spring and autumn, Via dei Coronari stages a prestigious Antiques Fair.

Restaurants

Antico Caffè della Pace

Via della Pace 3–7. Tel: (06) 6861216. £. Closed Mon. This old-fashioned café near Piazza Navona is popular with shoppers by day for tea or coffee. By night its bar is a popular haunt for wealthy young Romans.

Da Baffetto

Via del Governo Vecchio 11. Tel: (06) 6861617. £. Closed Sun and lunchtime. You will almost certainly have to queue for a table at this small, no-frills pizzeria – the most famous in Rome – but the scrumptious pizzas are well worth the wait.

Il Convivio

Via dell'Orso 44. Tel: (06) 6869432. £££. Closed Sun and lunchtime. The cosy mustard-coloured interior, the candle-lit tables, the creative, seasonal cuisine and a superb wine list are just some of the ingredients of a perfect evening at this, one of Rome's top restaurants.

Papa Giovanni

Via dei Sediari 4. Tel: (06) 6865308. Closed Sun and August. £££. Reservation essential. A classic Roman restaurant, serving traditional but refined Roman cuisine in an intimate setting.

Tre Scalini

Piazza Navona. ££. Closed Wed. You haven't experienced Rome until you have tasted the *tartufo* (truffle) ice-cream here, served in generous scoops and crowned with a dollop of whipped cream.

Caffè

Coffee drinking is something of a ritual in Rome, served in a variety of ways: caffè *(a regular black espresso);* caffè doppio *(a double);* capuccino *(half espresso, half frothy milk, topped with a sprinkling of cocoa);* caffè macchiato *(espresso with a drop of milk) and* caffè Hag *(decaffeinated). Try them all at* Sant'Eustachio *(* Piazza Sant' Eustachio 82, tel: (06) 6861309, closed Mon *), the café that reputedly serves the best cup of coffee in town.*

Nightlife

Winebars (*enotece*) abound in this district, notably romantic albeit pricey **La Bevitoria** in Piazza Navona (*closed Sun*), the aptly-named **Il Piccolo** (*Via del Governo Vecchio 74/75. Closed lunchtimes*), famous for its 'fruits of the forest' sangria, and **Cul de Sac** (*Piazza Pasquino, closed Sun*) with its staggering menu of over 1,400 different wines. Wild and wacky **Jonathan's Angels** (*Via della Fosse*) is another popular drinking venue, especially late at night. For live music, try sophisticated piano bar **Tartarughino** (*Via della Scrofa 1*) or the **Jazz Café** (*Piazza di Tor Sanguigna 12, open daily from 2230*). For something more cultural, occasional concerts at the Oratorio dei Filippini provide a chance to view the interior behind Borromini's celebrated façade, while the **Teatro Valle** (*Via di Teatro Valle 23, tel: (06) 68803794*) stages both Italian classic plays and lesser-known contemporary productions.

Shopping

Head to *Via del Governo Vecchio* for fashions, *Via dell' Orso* for jewellery, *Via degli Orsini* for antique lamps, *Via della Scrofa* for delicatessens *Volpetti* (No. 31/32) and *Antica Norcineria* (No. 100) and the famous *Via dei Coronari* for antiques. At the end of May and during October, Via dei Coronari holds its fair. The shops open late, the street is carpeted red and lined with candles, creating a truly magical atmosphere – ideal for an evening stroll.

Ai Monasteri

Piazza Cinque Lune 76. Monastic products from around Italy – fruit liqueurs, herbal concoctions, holy chocolates, honey, soaps and essential oils – crammed into a church-like shop.

Al Sogno

Piazza Navona 53. This toy shop is a favourite with children, with its giant cuddly animals, model cars, puppets, rocking horses and china dolls in lacy dresses.

Arsenale

Via del Governo Vecchio 64. Clothing for special occasions by local designer Patrizia Pieroni, accompanied by theatrical, Christian Lacroix-style accessories and a selection of hand-made shoes in a rainbow of colours.

Beatrice Palma

Via Pianellari 17. Want a piece of ancient Rome to take home? Come to this tiny workshop and select a plaster bust of Julius Caesar, a foot of Augustus or whatever takes your fancy!

In Folio

Corso V Emanuele II 261/263. Designer store with witty clocks, fun kitchenware, lava lamps, trendy gadgets and other 'accessories of the 21st century'.

Massimo Maria Melis

Via dell'Orso 57. Striking, highly exclusive jewellery inspired by traditional Roman and Etruscan designs, with a contemporary feel.

Aquatic Rome

*Rome is awash with fountains – over 4,000 in total –
more than any other city in the world. Among these are
some of the world's finest, the work of the greatest
sculptors of the Renaissance and Baroque. Some are
splashy, flamboyant displays, some are ornamental
trickles, many are simply humble drinking fountains.
You can drink the water from any of these fountains. It
is still as 'clear, sweet and fresh' as it was in Petrarch's
day, fed by mineral water running through the veins of
the city in giant aqueducts, 11 of which date from
Classical times.*

Papal splendour

The popes who restored these ancient aqueducts also adopted
the emperors' custom of celebrating the spot where the
water appears with a huge fountain or *mostra*
(show). The most famous is the Trevi Fountain,
immortalised by actress Anita Ekberg's late-
night dip in the film *La Dolce Vita*. Other
grand papal *mostre* include the Paola Fountain
on the Janiculum and the Moses Fountain on
Quirinal Hill.

Nearly all the great piazzas are graced with
fountains: Piazza Navona has Bernini's jewel of
Baroque sculpture, the Fountain of the Four
Rivers; Piazza Barberina has the Triton Fountain,
with its splendid sea god blowing through a
shell, and Piazza della Repubblica's sensual
Fountain of the Naiads caused a scandal when
it was unveiled in 1901, to reveal nymphs in
rather saucy postures.

Off the beaten track

Fountains of all shapes and sizes lie dotted about the city, some more unconventional than others. There's the Bee Fountain, the Frog Fountain, the Eagle Fountain, the Tortoise Fountain, *Facchino* the 'talking fountain', a water-clock fountain on Pincio hill, the modern Fountain of the Four Tiaras near St Peter's, the *Navicella* fountain, made from an ancient stone galley, *La Barcaccia* – a half-sunken barge at the foot of the Spanish Steps and the giant grotesque *Mascherone* face in Via Giulia, which in its Renaissance heyday flowed with wine, to name but a few.

Rome would be impossible to imagine without its fountains. Along with the car horn and the raised voices of passionate locals, the gentle splashing of water is one of Rome's distinguishing sounds.

Around Campo de' Fiori

Wedged between the Piazza Navona and the Tiber, this captivating corner of medieval Rome, with its intimate ochre squares and maze of twisting cobbled lanes and alleys, teems with market barrows, small boutiques, craft workshops and convivial cafés by day. By night, its sparkling squares buzz with atmosphere as locals and tourists alike pile into the trendy restaurants, cafés and clubs.

AROUND CAMPO DE' FIORI

*Getting there: **By bus:** Take Nos. 46, 62 or 64 which pass to the south of Piazza Navona along Corso Vittorio Emanuele II, or Nos. 70, 81, 87, 492 and 628, which pass to the east along Corso del Rinascimento, while No. 280 follows the course of the river around the northern perimeter of the district.*

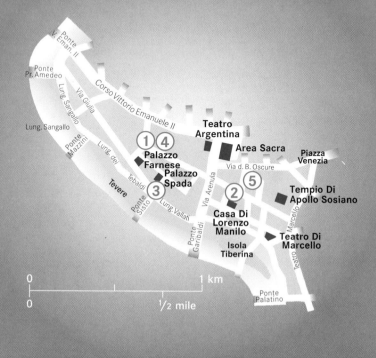

AROUND CAMPO DE' FIORI

① Campo de' Fiori

The 'Field of Flowers' was once a riverside meadow. Nowadays the bustling open-air morning food market offers a taste of the real Rome, its mouth-watering displays filling the air with intoxicating fragrances. This is the perfect place to stock up for a picnic or to try such special taste treats as salami, sun-dried tomatoes, marinated olives and artichokes. **Pages 62–63**

② Fontana delle Tartarughe

If you relish the discovery of a tiny, hidden *piazzetta*, surrounded by sun-baked terracotta houses and cooled by a gently splashing fountain, Piazza Mattei is definitely not to be missed; its delicate 'Tortoise Fountain' is considered one of the most delightful sights in Rome. **Page 64**

③ Shop 'til you drop

This district has for centuries been a popular place for shopping, with its ancient marketplace and tiny craft workshops in the maze of medieval streets named after the tailors, trunk makers, hatters and locksmiths who once lived here. Those with more expensive tastes should head for the sophisticated galleries and antiques shops which grace the Renaissance *palazzi* of Via Giulia. **Page 69**

④ Join the smart set

Join the smartly-dressed Romans meeting friends, eating and drinking or just posing in the animated bars and restaurants around Campo de' Fiori, currently the trendiest and most popular nightlife district in town. **Page 70**

⑤ Taste the delicious Jewish specialities

Be sure to taste some *filetti di baccalà* (deep fried salt cod), *carciofi alla giudia* (crisply-fried whole artichokes) and other such hearty Jewish-Roman recipes – trademarks of some of the city's finest traditional restaurants, hidden off the beaten track in the ancient Ghetto area. **Page 70**

Tip

The best time to visit Campo de' Fiori is during the morning market (weekdays only). But it is also fun to return again at lunchtime to watch the local market sellers packing up their stands and cleaning the square. Why not have a light lunch in one of the surrounding restaurants while you are there?

Tourist information

There are no tourist information booths in this district. The nearest ones are a short walk away at Piazza delle Cinque Lune, just north of Piazza Navona (*see page 45*) and at Piazza Sonnino in Trastevere (*see page 125*).

Area Sacra

Largo di Torre Argentina. Closed to the public.

The ruins of four pre-Christian temples were unearthed at this surprising venue – one of Rome's busiest junctions and a major bus interchange – as recently as 1929, in the course of an attempt to improve the road system. The oldest has been dated back to 300 BC, making it one of the city's most ancient monuments.

Although not open to the public, the ruins stand at Roman street level (several metres below today's level, due to centuries of accumulated dirt) making it easy to discern the outlines – three square and one round – of the temples from above. Little is known about the temples, so they are simply known as A, B, C and D, labelled from north to south. A is in the best condition; B in the centre, consecrated in 101 BC by Catulo, is the only round structure and boasts a mosaic floor; C is the oldest and the majority of D (apart from a section of the north wall dating from 200 BC) is covered by Via Florida. And don't miss the magnificent **public toilets** – just behind temple A and best viewed from Via di Torre Argentina – unpartitioned so that the toga-clad citizens of ancient Rome could use the time fruitfully, discussing the news and gossip of the day!

Campo de' Fiori

Campo de' Fiori is one of the trendiest parts of Rome, lively day and night. On weekdays at crack of dawn, the 'Field of Flowers' bursts into life as market workers prepare their stalls ready for **Rome's finest market** (*Mon–Fri 0600–1300*). Come rain or shine, under giant multi-coloured *ombrellone* (umbrellas) are dazzling displays of fruit, flowers, fish, salami, sun-dried tomatoes, olives, artichokes, pesto, peppers, roughly-cut hunks of Parmesan and all the tastes, fragrances and colours of Italian cuisine – a veritable feast for the senses. By night, cafés, bars and restaurants fill the piazza, making it one of Rome's most animated night spots.

However, the atmosphere in the square has not always been so bustling and cheerful. Campo de' Fiori was used as an execution ground by the Popes until well into modern times. The **sombre black sculpture** overseeing the square today is of Giordano Bruno, a famous Renaissance monk and philosopher, who was burned at the stake here in 1600 by the Counter-Reformation papacy for his belief that the earth moved around the sun and was therefore not the centre of the universe.

Casa di Lorenzo Manilo

Via del Portico d'Ottavia 1. Closed to the public.

Lorenzo Manilo's bold terracotta-orange house at the heart of the Ghetto district boasts one of Rome's most unusual façades. Thanks to the Renaissance revival of interest in history and the arts, it became fashionable to build houses recalling the splendour of ancient Rome. Manilio decided to renovate his family home in 1468 by adding pieces of **original Roman reliefs** from the Via Appia Antica (*see pages 161–162*). Look closely and you will see a sculpted row of Roman busts, a lion and deer carving from an

ancient sarcophagus and *Ave Roma* (Hail Rome) patriotically engraved above the windows. His finishing touch – a broad, sand-coloured **Classical plaque** – dates the building according to the ancient Roman calendar, 2,221 years after the founding of Rome in 753 BC.

> ❝ Here and there one sees a fine orange ochre that has retained a warm glow, a serene density, beneath its slowly acquired patina. ❞
>
> **Valéry Larbaud,**
> *Aux couleurs de Rome*

Fontana della Tartarughe

Piazza Mattei.

The exquisite 'Tortoise Fountain' is one of Rome's best-loved. It depicts four cavorting male nymphs, each grasping in one hand a dolphin jetting water into marble shells, whilst with the other hand gently lifting a tortoise to drink from the fountain's upper basin. This charming scene was sculpted by **Tadeo Landini** in just one night in 1585 – a rushed commission by the Duke of Mattei who, a compulsive gambler, had lost all his money and consequently his fiancée, and wanted to prove to her father that he was still worthy of her hand. The bronze tortoises – a finishing touch of genius – were actually added a century later, possibly by Bernini.

Ghetto

From just north of Via del Portico d'Ottavia (the main street) to the Tiber and from Via Arenula to via Teatro di Marcello.

Rome's Jewish community is considered Europe's oldest, in continuous existence for over 2,000 years. Despite arriving originally as slaves, most Jewish settlers were honest merchants attracted to the hub of the Empire, and respected for their financial and business skills. Their systematic persecution began under Pope Paul IV who in 1556 forced them all to live and work in a small, unhealthy and frequently flooded district within a high-walled enclosure. They were allowed out by day, but the gates were locked at night. They had to wear yellow hats to distinguish them from Christians and on Sundays were forced to attend Christian services at **Sant' Angelo in Pescheria** (*see page 67*), a practice only abolished in 1848 when the walls of the Ghetto were finally torn down.

In 1874, Rome's Jewish community built a massive new Synagogue (*Lungotevere dei Cenci; open Mon–Thur 0930–1700, 1800 in summer; Fri 0930–1330, 1700 in summer; Sun 0930–1230; closed Sat; admission: £*) in travertine marble with an imposing aluminium dome in Assyrian-Babylonian style. On the river side **a plaque** commemorates the hundreds of Roman Jews persecuted yet again under Fascism during World War II, many deported to German concentration camps, never to return. Next to the Synagogue is the **Jewish Museum**

> *As we move about the Rome of to-day, we may find it hard to believe in her old magnificence.*
>
> **Mark Twain**

Today the Ghetto area lacks any architectural unity, but many Jews still live here. The medieval streets retain much of their old character with their Jewish bakery, bookshop, kosher food stores and restaurants serving hearty Jewish-Roman cuisine, making it a truly fascinating district to explore.

Palazzo Farnese

French Embassy, Piazza Farnese. Closed to the public.

This is the most splendid of all Rome's Renaissance palaces, built for the Farnese family, one of the most powerful in the city. Just about every famous 16th-century Roman architect lent a hand in its lengthy construction (1514–89), including da Sangallo, Michelangelo and della Porta. The finished result is surprisingly austere, its monumental yet neat façade so devoid of decoration that the Romans nickname it *il dado* (the dice). Its real gems lie hidden inside – try to get a peep of the **stunning arcaded courtyard** and the dazzling ceiling frescoes by Carracci.

Outside, the spacious, grand Piazza Farnese's jolly pavement cafés and restaurants are cooled by **twin fountains** – their jets of water splashing from giant lilies (the emblem of the Farnese family) into ancient marble bathtubs from the Baths of Caracalla.

Palazzo Spada

Via Capo di Ferro 3. Tel: (06) 6861158. Open Tue–Sat 0900–1900; Sun 0900–1300. Closed Mon. Admission: ££.

Don't miss this palace – it has the most ornate façade in all of Rome. Built for a wealthy cardinal in 1550 and later acquired by the Spada family in 1632, it is smothered in exuberant stucco Mannerist decorations (attributed to Giulio Mazzoni) with eight niches containing statues of ancient Romans, including Marcellus and Caesar.

Cardinal Spada amassed a fine collection of paintings, including works by Rubens, Tintoretto, Guercino, Dürer and Reni – one of the best patrician art collections in Rome. The **courtyard** contains fanciful reliefs of such mythological figures as Venus, Mars and Pluto together with posing Carabinieri, standing guard in their trendy sunglasses to protect the Italian Council of State, also housed here. Look out also for Borromini's ingenious **corridor** in the east garden, with its cunning *trompe l'oeil* perspective. A long colonnade stretches out to a large statue at the end. Walk along it and you will discover that the colonnade is only a quarter of the length it seems and that the statue, placed against a painted garden backdrop, is actually pint-sized.

Portico d'Ottavia

Via del Portico d'Ottavia

The Portico of Octavia must be one of the city's least-visited ruins. Built by Quintus Metellus in 146 BC, it was renovated by Augustus in 27 BC and dedicated to his sister Octavia, as part of an imperial covered passageway linking the Teatro di Pompey and the Teatro di Marcello (*see page 68*). All that remains today is the *propylaeum*, or entrance, which originally fronted a huge double colonnade of 300 columns with a library, twin temples and countless statues within its confines.

In the Middle Ages, a covered fish market and church – Sant' Angelo in Percheria (The Angel of the Fishmongers) – were built in the ruins of the Portico. Look closely and you can still see a **Latin inscription** regulating fish measurements.

Teatro Argentina

Largo di Torre Argentina 52. Tel: (06) 68804601 for performance details and tickets.

The Argentina Theatre was built in 1731, over the vast ruins of Pompey's Theatre (61 BC), the first permanent theatre building in Rome. It is thought to mark the spot where Julius Caesar was stabbed to death by a group of senators on the Ides of March in 44 BC.

> " *To begin with, Rossini decides to wear a bigogna suit … this colour provokes general laughter in the audience … Figaro appears with his mandoline; as soon as he touches it all the strings break. Enter Basile and he falls on his nose … The stamping and the hoots cover the sound of the orchestra and the voices; Rossini leaves the piano and runs for the safety of his home behind lock and key.* "

The première of *The Barber of Seville*, (Stendhal, *Promenades dans Rome*)

Today Teatro Argentina is home to the prestigious **Teatro di Roma** repertory company and the official centre of theatre in Rome, staging plays, concerts and international theatre festivals, with the occasional performance in English. Over the years it has witnessed the premières of many great operas. However, the opening night of Rossini's *Barber of Seville* in 1816 was a disaster. Apparently Napoleon's sister, Pauline Borghese, was furious with Rossini for not reworking the tenor part for her friend and had packed the house with hecklers (*see above*). Following the second performance, a more sincere audience went *en masse* by torchlight to Rossini's house to show their appreciation of his masterwork.

Teatro di Marcello

Via del Teatro di Marcello. Closed except for concerts (contact the tourist office for details).

The Theatre of Marcellus is one of the most intriguing of all Rome's ruins, with its various layers of history one on top of the other. Julius Caesar began its construction, in an attempt to upstage Pompey, whose own theatre was just being completed nearby. It was finished in 23 BC by Augustus, who dedicated it to his recently deceased son-in-law and heir, 19-year-old Marcellus. However, serious theatre never really caught on, so both venues were used for more fashionable, bloodthirsty sporting events.

Round virtually every corner in the centro storico *lie treasures of ancient history – an Etruscan pillar here, a Roman statue there! The three Corinthian columns just north of the Teatro di Marcello were once part of the Temple of Apollo (500 BC), which housed Rome's most precious artworks plundered from Greece in 200 BC.*

Almost half of the **theatre's ruins** are still visible. The other half was gradually demolished, first in the fourth century AD to repair the Ponte Cestio, then in the 12th century, to build a massive fortress for the Savelli family on top of the ruins. Subsequently, over the years rich papal families built their waterfront palaces here, all on top of the original theatre. The lower arches were occupied by more humble dwellings and shops until as recently as 1932. Nowadays, the upper storeys of these Renaissance ruins contain fashionable, well-appointed apartments.

Isola Tiberina

Before you cross onto Tiber Island via **Ponte Fabricio** (62 BC) – the oldest bridge in the city still in use – take a good look at its shape. The ancient Romans built large structures of white travertine at either end to make it resemble the stern and prow of a ship. In 293 BC they dedicated a temple here to Aesculapius, the Greek god of healing, who supposedly sent one of his serpents by ship to rid Rome of the plague. Ever since, the serpent entwined around Aesculapius' staff has become a world-acknowledged medical symbol, and the island has been associated with the

sick. **Fatebenefratelli Hospital** occupies the entire upstream side of the island while the River Police (whose work includes recovering bodies from the Tiber and rescuing those who fall or jump in) have their quarters at the other end ... in the old city morgue!

On a more cheery note, the island boasts great views of the 'Tiber of the blue water, the river most dear to heaven' (Virgil), an excellent restaurant (The Sora Lella), the charming Romanesque church of **San Bartolomeo** and **Pierleoni-Caetani Castle**, one of Rome's most important medieval monuments, which contains the Tiber Island History Museum (currently closed for restoration work).

Via Giulia

Imagine Via Giulia in its heyday! It was laid out in 1508 by Pope Julius II (hence the name) as the main route from Rome to St Peter's – long, straight and narrow in stark contrast with the surrounding maze of winding, medieval lanes. It immediately became the fashionable place to live, with many of the papal elite building sumptuous palaces along it (as did wealthy artists such as Cellini and Raphael) and it was *the* venue for parties in Rome. On one occasion, wine gushed from the **Mascherone Fountain** for three full days! Nowadays, this stunning street – still flanked by magnificent Renaissance palazzi at every turn – is quiet and largely-traffic free, but it remains a prestigious address especially for upmarket antique shops and art galleries (*see page 71*).

Restaurants

Al 16

Via del Portico d'Ottavia 16. Tel: (06) 6874722. ££. Closed Tue. One of several traditional Jewish restaurants in Rome, serving copious quantities of *carciofi alla giudia* (Jewish-style artichokes), *filetti di baccala* (fried salt-cod fillets) and *fiori di zucca* (stuffed courgette flowers).

Ar Galletto/Da Giovanni

Vicolo del Gallo 1/Piazza Farnese 102. Tel: (06) 6861714. ££. Closed Sun and part of August. A jolly, atmospheric restaurant serving straightforward home-cooking in one of Rome's loveliest squares.

Filetti di Baccalà

Largo dei Librari 88. Tel: (06) 6864018. £. Closed lunchtimes. Roman fish and chips to take away wrapped in paper, or to eat at formica tables with a carafe of *vino della casa*.

Da Giggetto

Via del Portico d'Ottavia 21a. Tel: (06) 6561105. ££. Closed Mon. Typical Jewish-style trattoria hung with strings of garlic, sage and chillies, serving hearty Roman cuisine in a homely atmosphere.

Ditirambo

Piazza della Cancelleria 74/75. Tel: (06) 6871626. Closed Mon. ££–£££. Booking recommended. A small restaurant with unusual dishes, delicious home-baked bread, fine wines and friendly waiters.

Hostaria Costanza

Piazza Paradiso 63/65. Tel: (06) 6861717. ££–£££. Closed Sun and August. Booking recommended. This traditional Roman restaurant is built under the remains of the ancient Teatro Pompeo where Julius Caesar was stabbed to death by Brutus and friends on the Ides of March in 44 BC ... but don't let that put you off your meal!

La Taverna degli Amici

Piazza Margana 36/7. Tel: (06) 69920637. Closed Mon. A romantic restaurant with checked table-cloths and candles, set in a pretty Baroque piazza, and serving wholesome country fare. Be sure to save room for the divine desserts!

Nightlife

This is a youthful, late-night party area with a wide choice of bars and pubs, some with a disco atmosphere. Popular bars such as the **Drunken Ship** (*Piazza Campo de' Fiori 20*) and its more traditional neighbour **Enoteca Vineria** (*No. 15, closed Sun*) are always crowded both before and after dinner, while **Crazy Bull** (*Via Mantova 5b*) an American-style disco-bar, and *birrerie* **Mad Jack** (*Via Arenula 20*) are more late-night venues.

Campo de' Fiori also hosts the **Teatro Argentina**, formerly an opera house, but now home of Rome's main theatre repertory company.

Shopping

For centuries this district has been home to craftsmen, furniture restorers and artists, and it is easy to pass many an hour browsing in the small workshops and boutiques of Via Giulia, Via Monserrato, Via Pellegrino and Via dei Cappellari for arts, crafts, antiques and furnishings.

Antichi Ferri Italiani
Via Giulia 86. Tel: (06) 68136632. A small, exclusive shop specialising in antique wrought-ironwork.

Atlanta
Piazza Mattei 13. Tel: (06) 6865513. This wacky shop, by the turtle fountain, is full of quality souvenirs and novel gift ideas – glass jewellery, silk scarves, jazzy ceramics, even pottery Vespas.

Galeria Farnese
Piazza Farnese. Tel: (06) 6896109. If you wish to purchase part of an original tiled floor from Palazzo Venezia or part of a Roman bath, visit this extraordinary Aladdin's cave of beautiful antique tiles, jars, urns and marble.

Handles
Via delle Pettinari 53. Tel: (06) 68803119. Knobs and knockers of all shapes and sizes from shiny brass lions' heads to pink, plastic hearts.

Loco
Via dei Baullari. Romans hot-foot it here for the latest in trendy, original shoe designs.

Picnic supplies

For a picnic made in heaven, supplement your purchases at the market in Piazza Campo de' Fiori with bread from Il Forno (No. 22), cold cuts from Norchineria Viola (No. 43) and wine, cheese, olives and anchovies from Salsamantaria Ruggeri.

PROFILE

Patronage and the arts

The majority of significant buildings in the centro storico *stand today as historic expressions of an*

increasingly powerful church or as reminders of the city's leading dynastic families, the great patrons of the arts who would commission the top artists and architects of the day to create fine palaces, paintings, piazzas, fountains, chapels and churches as symbols of their power, wealth and prestige. According to the Renaissance Pope Nicholas V, there were few better ways to impress than 'outstanding sights… great buildings… and divine monuments'.

The Renaissance

Unlike Florence, Rome cannot lay claim to the Renaissance – the great 're-birth' of interest in the arts. However, papal patronage acted as a powerful magnet, drawing the cream of Florentine artists – Michelangelo, Raphael, Fra Angelico, Lippi and Botticelli – southwards to take their inspiration from the city's Classical ruins, while local prodigy **Bramante** worked on the designs for St Peter's. **Raphael** arrived in 1508 to decorate the Vatican apartments of Julius II while **Michelangelo**, best known for his *Last Judgement* in the Sistine Chapel commissioned by Pope Paul III, also left a

legacy of designs throughout the city including the Campidoglio and Palazzo Farnese.

The Baroque

The Baroque found its strongest flowering in Rome. No other architectural period left a more lasting stamp on the city than the 17th-century fascination for the exuberantly theatrical. Yet without the patronage of the papacy, whose increasing power and prosperity enabled them to dictate fashion, the Baroque era would probably never have happened. Leading patrons of this period, notably Barberini Pope Urban VIII, were quick to realise the genius of such men as **Borromini**, **Caravaggio** and **Cortona**, and in just a few years countless churches were remodelled with lavish decoration, and piety sought through dramatic, emotive artworks and extravagant *trompe l'oeil* ceilings. Monumental family palaces sprung up and piazzas were adorned with extravagant fountains.

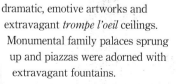

However, the real artistic dictator of Rome was **Bernini**, sponsored for over 20 years by the wealthy Barberini family. He alone virtually created the Baroque. Through such masterworks as Piazza Navona and *The Ecstasy of St Teresa* he changed the face of Rome, giving brilliant expression to a style later to be imitated throughout Europe.

73

Around Piazza della Rotonda

No other neighbourhood is quite like this. The centuries have left an extraordinary variety of sights including the remarkable Pantheon, stately Renaissance palazzi and ebulliently Baroque churches. Yet alongside these tourist 'must-sees', its narrow, winding streets and tiny sun-baked piazzas hide a multitude of lesser-known surprises including the enormous foot of a marble Roman giant, the oldest cat in town and the very best gelaterie.

AROUND PIAZZA DELLA ROTONDA

BEST OF

Piazza della Rotonda

Getting there: **By bus:** *Electric minibus 116 whizzes along the twisting streets surrounding Piazza della Rotonda following a circular route between Via Veneto and Campo de' Fiori. Otherwise regular buses ply the main thoroughfares with Nos. 46, 62 and 64 to the south along Corso Vittorio Emanuele II, Nos. 70, 81, 87, 492 and 628 on Corso del Rinascimento to the west, and Nos. 56, 60, 61, 62, 81, 85, 95, 160, 492 and 628 to the east on Via del Corso.*

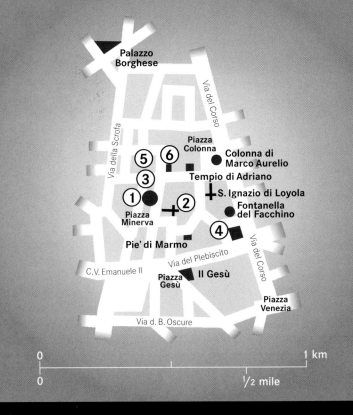

AROUND PIAZZA DELLA ROTONDA

① Pantheon

Created in 17 BC, the Pantheon is indisputably the best-preserved major monument of Imperial Rome and a marvel of ancient architecture. If possible, visit it during a storm to experience the rain splashing straight onto the colourful original marble flooring! **Pages 80–81**

② Trompe l'oeil treasures

The dozen or so churches in this area provide sanctuary from the noisy outside world, and a cool retreat from the blazing midsummer sun. Don't miss Rome's only Gothic church, Santa Maria sopra Minerva, or the astonishing *trompe l'oeil* ceiling frescoes in the Jesuit churches, Il Gesù and Sant' Ignazio di Loyola. **Page 85**

③ Soak up the sun

Fountain-splashed Piazza della Rotonda is the liveliest piazza in the neighbourhood, and a great place to dally over a coffee or a refreshing *granita di limone* in one of several cafés overlooking the Pantheon. **Page 86**

④ Appreciate fine art

Palazzo-Galleria Doria Pamphilj contains one of Rome's best surviving private collections of art, with canvases by Titian, Caravaggio, Velasquez and Raphael among others. An absolute must for art lovers! **Page 83**

⑤ Try the best ice-cream in Rome ...

This district is heaven for ice-cream fans, boasting the finest *gelaterie*. Choose from row upon mouth-watering row of divine flavours in Caffè della Palma or tuck into an old-fashioned ice-cream sundae at Caffè Giolitti, the best-known *gelateria* in town. **Page 86**

⑥ ... and the best espresso!

According to the Romans, tiny Sant' Eustachio café (*see page 54*) serves the best cup of coffee in town ... and, given the number of cups the average Roman drinks per day, they should know. However, La Tazza d'Oro is a strong rival for the Roman coffee crown. **Page 86**

Tip

Electric minibus 116 is ideal for those in a hurry (or with weary limbs!). It passes close by such sights as Palazzo Borghese, the Pantheon, Piazza della Rotonda, Sant' Ignazio di Loyola, the Temple of Hadrian and the column of Marcus Aurelius.

Tourist information

There is a tourist information booth at Largo Carlo Goldoni, just off the Corso. *Open daily 0900–1800 (tel: (06) 68136061).*

Colonna di Marco Aurelio

Piazza Colonna.

It is the realism of the carvings on this ancient monument that makes it so striking. Built between 180 and 196 AD to commemorate the victories of Marcus Aurelius over Germanic tribes and the Sarmatians, it emulates the Column of Trajan (*see page 30*) with its spiral bands portraying battle scenes in relief. However, these images accentuate the horrors of war rather than the glory. Note the **terror-stricken faces** of the desperately beseeching barbarians and the way in which **Marcus Aurelius** is sculpted mostly face-on, making him appear more stately.

The column's surroundings are also worth a look. **Piazza Colonna** is one of Rome's main squares, flanked by two important 17th-century palaces. On the north side, **Palazzo Chigi** is the official residence of the Prime Minister. Neighbouring **Palazzo Montecitorio** houses the Italian Parliament. Peaceful and pedestrianised by night, by day the square is frequently filled with gesticulating politicians, TV film crews and diplomats and ministers in speeding blue Lancias.

Fontanella del Facchino

Via Lata.

This weathered fountain of a man holding a cask, known to locals as Il Facchino (The Porter) was one of the city's notorious 16th-century 'talking fountains' (*see Pasquino, page 49*). His origins remain a mystery: some say he is modelled on Martin Luther or, more likely, a drawing of the Fraternity of Water-carriers by Florentine painter Jacopino del Conte; others claim 'The Porter' was a celebrated drunk who died whilst staggering around with a barrel!

Il Gesù

Piazza del Gesù. Open daily 0630–1230, 1600–1915. Admission: £.

The Gesù was the first church built in Rome for the Jesuits, a Roman Catholic order founded by the Basque soldier and saint, Ignatius Loyola in 1534. Its design, completed in 1584, represents the epitome of Counter-Reformation Baroque architecture: its austere façade by della Porta typifies the serious religious demands of the Catholic Church at this tricky time of Protestant revolt against Rome; its **spacious interior** by Vignola enabled preaching to huge congregations, with the main altar visible throughout so that all could follow Mass. This style became known as the 'Jesuit Style' and has since been widely copied throughout the Catholic world.

Don't let the dull, grimy exterior of the church put you off entering, because the interior is surprisingly lavish. This is thanks to Jesuit general Fra Olivia in the late 17th century, who decided that the church should reflect the triumph of the Order, and therefore turned to Rome's most prestigious artists and craftsmen. The altar in the **Chapel of St Ignatius** (in the left transept) is the work of Jesuit artist Andrea del Pozzo – an exuberant Baroque confection of gold, bronze and coloured marble, considered the most valuable altar in Christendom. It shows the apparition of the Trinity to St Ignatius (who lies buried beneath it) and includes a globe carried by angels that is the largest piece of lapis lazuli in the world.

Windy quarter

Piazza del Gesù is said to be the windiest square in Rome. According to an old Roman story, the Devil was out walking with the Wind one day. As they passed Il Gesù, the Devil decided to pop into the church for a while. He never came out and to this day the Wind waits for him, still swirling around the busy piazza.

The real *pièce de resistance* of the Gesù, however, is the exultant *trompe l'oeil* ceiling by **Il Baciccio** – *The Adoration of the Name of Jesus* (1674) – one of the most influential frescoes of the High Baroque. Its message is simple: it portrays faithful Catholics being welcomed into Heaven through a hole in the clouds, while Protestants and other heretics (spilling over the edges of the painting onto the coffered vaulting of the nave) are flung into the fires of hell.

Pantheon

The impact on visitors of the best-preserved monument of ancient Rome is so striking that the Pantheon is considered one of the great symbols of Rome. Even in imperial times, when this district was packed with grand gardens, a lagoon, the Minerva temple, the Circus of Domitian, the Theatre of Pompey and other magnificent public buildings, the Pantheon was the centrepiece.

Founded by Augustus' general, Marcus Agrippa in AD 17 as a 'temple of all the gods' (hence the inscription mentioning *Agrippa* on the pediment, which confused historians for centuries!), it received its present-day appearance 100 years later, under Hadrian. The building's astonishing state of preservation is due to its conversion to a Christian church in 608 – the church of **Santa Maria ad Martyres**. It remains officially a church today (although services are seldom held), and is probably the place of origin of the Festival of All Saints.

Perfect symmetry

One of the most striking features of the Pantheon is the way it fuses the Greek *pronaos* (porch) of a temple with the

Roman domed *rotunda*. The key to its harmony and striking simplicity is its dimensions. From the outside the dome looks saucer-shaped, but inside you will discover that it is a perfect hemisphere and that the diameter of the **interior dome** is exactly equal to the height of the building. It is a remarkable feat of Roman engineering – the largest vault ever constructed in stone (even the dome of St Peter's is smaller) – with 6m-thick walls, constructed by pouring concrete, tufa and pumice over a temporary wooden framework. The only source of light is a circular gaping hole (*oculus*) in the roof, a symbolic link between the temple and the heavens.

Memorials to the famous

Inside, numerous eminent Italians lie buried, from the first kings of united Italy to **Raphael**, whose mistress and model La Fornarina, with whom he had lived for many years, was banned from his funeral – probably because the artist was engaged for many years to the niece of his patron, whose memorial is just to the right of the 37-year-old artist's tomb.

From temple to market-square

" This open and secret temple [The Pantheon] was conceived as a sundial. The hours were to circle the centre of its carefully polished pavement, where the disk of the day was supposed to rest like a golden buckler; there the rain would make a limpid pool from which prayer could transpire like smoke toward the void where we place the gods. "

Marguerite Yourcenar,
Memoirs of Hadrian

On leaving the Pantheon, note the original Roman bronze doors. The roof was also once entirely clad in bronze, part of which was stripped as early as 667. The remainder was melted down in the 1620s and used by Bernini to construct the great baldacchino over the high altar in St Peter's (*see pages 146–147*). The **portico** was used as a market until the 18th century. Look closely at the 16 colossal columns that support the triangular gable, and you will see notches in the granite that used to support the market-stalls. The fountain-splashed **Piazza della Rotonda**, enlivened by countless cafés, makes a perfect (albeit pricey) venue to while away the hours over an *espresso* or *granita*, and marvel at this great treasure of Roman antiquity.

Getting there: Piazza della Rotonda. Open daily 0900–1830 (1600 in winter); Sun 0900–1300. Admission: £.

Palazzo Borghese

Largo della Fontanella di Borghese. Closed to the public.

Due to its unusual ground-plan, this delightful 17th-century palazzo is known as the 'harpsichord of Rome', with its curvaceous façade as *la tastiera* (the keyboard). It was purchased in 1605 by Camillo Borghese (the future Pope Paul V) and his flamboyant wife, Pauline Bonaparte, Napoleon's sister. Before long, the palace became famous for the extravagant parties and concerts held on its riverside terrace. But Pauline hated it, complaining that it was cold, damp and had no bathroom!

For over two centuries, Palazzo Borghese housed the family's renowned art collection, (now in Villa Borghese (*see pages 162–165*). Today it contains the Spanish Embassy and is closed to the public. Nonetheless, try to get at least a glimpse into the **porticoed inner courtyard** (best viewed from Via dell'Arancio) with its marvellous statuary and fountains, including Rainaldi's charming Rococo *Bath of Venus*. On the other side of the palazzo, **Largo della Fontanella di Borghese** is the site of a picturesque market of old books, maps, paintings and prints (*open Mon–Sat morning only*).

Palazzo-Galleria Doria Pamphilj

Piazza del Collegio Romano 2. Tel: (06) 6797323; open Fri–Wed 1000–1700, closed Thur and 15 Aug. Admission: £££. Tours of the private apartments (in Italian only) from 1030–1230. Admission: ££. www.doriapamphilj.it.

Cats

The tiny marble cat (gatta) perched on a cornice of a building beside Palazzo Doria-Pamphilj, on the otherwise unremarkable Via della Gatta, is a must-see for all cat lovers! It used to be part of Emperor Domitian's Temple of Isis, making it the oldest feline in a city of a million cats, who over the years have made such ancient sites as the Forum and the Area Sacra their home.

This impressive palazzo belonging to the great pillar of Rome's aristocracy, the Doria-Pamphilj family, contains the best private patrician art collection in Rome, with over 400 paintings (predominantly Italian) from the 15th century to the 18th century, including canvases by Titian, Caravaggio, Jan Breughels and Guercino. There are too many fine works to digest in one visit, but don't miss **Raphael's** sombre *Double Portrait of two Venetians* and **Velázquez's** portrait of the Pamphilj Pope Innocent X, displayed alongside a bust of the same pontiff by Bernini. Innocent X was, of course, Bernini's patron.

Once inside the palace, its sheer size, occupying an entire street block, will become apparent, as will a cacophony of architectural styles hidden behind the Rococo façade, following centuries of possession by the Doria-Pamphilj family who still live here today. The private apartments, containing family treasures amassed over the centuries, are well worth viewing, especially the grand **Ballroom**, the English-style **Smoking Room** (built for a homesick British bride), the **Yellow Room** with superb Brussels and Gobelin tapestries and the **Winter Garden**, with its antique board games and charming children's sledge.

Pie' di Marmo

Via del Pie' di Marmo.

A giant marble foot … surely one of the strangest remains of ancient Rome! You will find it firmly planted on the corner of Via Pie'di Marmo (literally 'street of the marble foot') and Via Santo Stefano del Cacco. During the Roman Empire, the entire city was dotted with giant statues of gods and emperors, gloriously painted by their supporters and adorned with clothes and jewels. This particular district was dedicated to the Egyptian gods Isis and Serapis, so the foot is almost certainly part of a statue from one of their temples.

Santa Maria Sopra Minerva (and Obelisk)

Piazza della Minerva 42. Open daily 0700–1200, 1600–1900. Admission: £.

Of the 901 churches in Rome, Santa Maria sopra Minerva is the sole Gothic example. Built in 1280 on the site of an ancient temple of Minerva, it is attributed to the architects of Florence's great Santa Maria Novella, Fra Ristoro and Fra Sisto of the Dominican Order to which both churches belong.

The spacious **interior**, with its Gothic crossbeam vaulting, was restored in the 19th century and quirkily painted midnight blue with gold stars. It boasts numerous **fine tombs** and treasures, thanks to various wealthy families who financed funerary chapels and art works over the centuries. Buried under the altar is **St Catherine of Siena**, the patron saint of Rome who died in the Dominican convent here in 1380. Just to the left, the simple tomb of the great Florentine artist and Dominican monk **Fra Angelico** contrasts poignantly with the lavish tombs of Medici popes **Leo X** and **Clement VII** in the apse. These two Renaissance popes contributed considerably to the decoration of the church, including the commissioning of *Christ bearing the Cross* by Michelangelo (1520), an emotive sculpture full of the artist's characteristic intensity. The second chapel of the right transept, smothered in magnificent Lippi frescoes, contains the tomb of the infamous Carafa **Pope Paul IV** – the bloodiest, most

Elephant

The statue outside the church of an elephant carrying the smallest obelisk in Rome was designed by Bernini in 1666 for Pope Alexander VII. It is undoubtedly one of the city's most charming sculptures, frequently nicknamed 'il pulcin' della Minerva' (Minerva's baby).

reviled pope of all and father of the Inquisition, mainly remembered for his persecution of Jews. Less well-known is the fact that he ordered an incongruous bronze loincloth to be added to Michelangelo's marble sculpture of Christ in Santa Maria sopra Minerva. And worse still … he made Daniele da Volterra paint loincloths on all the nudes in Michelangelo's *Last Judgement* (*see page 145*)!

Sant' Ignazio di Loyola

Piazza di Sant' Ignazio; open daily 0730–1230, 1600–1900. Admission: £.

This church is set in one of Rome's most original squares – a highly original late Baroque ensemble of curvy buildings with frivolously decorated façades which looks more like a stage set than a piazza. It provides the perfect counterbalance to the sombre, imposing façade of the church, which was designed by a Jesuit architect, Padre Orazio Grassi in 1626 to celebrate the canonisation of the Jesuit founder, Ignatius of Loyola (*see page 79*).

The severe exterior belies the dizzying splendour of the extravagantly **gilded interior**, which in turn is dominated by one of Rome's most **famous ceilings**, *The Entry of St Ignatius into Paradise* by Andrea Pozzo – a remarkable *trompe l'oeil* portrayal of heaven. He also contributed the dome – not a real dome as there was not enough money, but rather a flat disc of paint made to look like one (best viewed from a yellow disk in the middle of the nave).

Tempio di Adriano

Piazza di Pietra.

This is one of Rome's many rarely-noticed treasures of antiquity – 11 massive Corinthian columns, originally part of a temple built to honour Emperor Hadrian by his adopted son and successor, Antonius Pius in 145 AD. These chunky granite columns are embedded in the wall of the Roman **stock exchange** (virtually inactive today, as the main Italian Borsa is now in Milan). Further treasures salvaged from the temple are displayed in the courtyard of the Palazzo dei Conservatori (*see page 25*).

Eating and drinking

This is one of the most densely populated areas of Rome for cafés, bars and restaurants.

Il Bacaro

Via degli Spagnoli 27. Tel: (06) 6864110. Closed Sun and lunchtimes in winter. ££. A charming candlelit restaurant near the Pantheon, popular with the young set, especially in summer with its picturesque terrace.

Caffè di Rienzo

Piazza della Rotonda 9. Tel: (06) 6869097. Closed Mon. Enjoy the speciality *granita di limone* (frozen, crushed lemon juice accompanied by a silver pitcher of water to adjust the sharpness) on this sunny terrace overlooking the Pantheon.

Cíao

Via del Corso/Via Convertite. No tel. £. Italian fast food at its best – generous slices of take-away pizza at absurdly cheap prices, combined with a cheap, cheerful self-service restaurant at the back. Excellent value.

Da Gino

Vicolo Rossini 4. Tel: (06) 6873434. ££. Closed Sun. Reservation recommended. This lively, brightly-lit trattoria serves up wholesome soups, steaks and mixed grills *all'italiana* as well as traditional Italian dishes.

Giolitti

Via Uffici del Vicario 40. Tel: (06) 6991243. £. Closed Mon. This olde-worlde *gelateria*-cum-teashop boasts arguably the best ice-cream in Rome, served in chocolate-rimmed cones, not to mention their moreish sundaes, cakes and pastries.

Quinze e Gabrielli

Via delle Copelle 6. Tel: (06) 6879389. £££. Reservation essential. Rome's top fish restaurant. The décor resembles a group of tropical islands, with palm trees and gazebos. Even the table-cloths are sand-coloured. For a special treat, try the sea-date soup followed by Sardinian spiny lobster.

La Tazza d'Oro

Via degli Orfani 86. Tel: (06) 6789792. Closed Sun. As the name suggests, 'the Cup of Gold' – a stand-up café-bar-cum-shop – sells only coffee, and rivals Caffè Sant' Eustachio (*see page 54*) for Rome's best cuppa. It is also famed for its *granita di caffè con panna* – a delicious concoction of frozen coffee and whipped cream.

El Toulà

Via della Lupa 29b. Tel: (06) 6873498. £££. Closed Sun and August. Reservation essential. Sophisticated Venetian and international cuisine in a flower-filled, elegant environment, El Toulà is considered by many Rome's number one restaurant.

Shopping

This district offers an excellent variety of shopping from the inexpensive, mid-range clothes, shoes and accessories shops of Via del Corso, one of the city's most popular shopping streets famed for its evening passeggiata *(see page 9), to the quaint antique books and prints market outside Palazzo Borghese (see pages 162–165) and the clutter of tiny specialist boutiques near the Pantheon, most notably Via dei Cestari, lined with shops supplying the ecclesiastical population with silver chalices, candles and crimson cardinals' socks.*

Cartoleria Pantheon

Via della Rotonda 15. A tiny treasure-trove of hand-made, marbled paper items – writing paper, wrapping paper, notelets, notebooks, diaries and beautiful leather-bound photo albums.

Confetteria Moriondo e Gariglio

Via del Pie'di Marmo 21/22. On Valentine's Day and for Easter, Romans queue outside the city's only family-run chocolate confectioners to have their special gifts sealed inside beautifully-wrapped chocolate hearts and eggs.

Curiosita e Magica

Piazza Montecitorio 70. Stepping inside this extraordinary, old-fashioned magic shop is like entering another world, full of magic, sorcery and tricks. An experience not to be missed!

La Rinascente

Via del Corso 189. Rome's most upmarket department store, stocking designer and off-the-peg fashions for men and women, lingerie, costume jewellery and accessories.

Gelati

It would be a crime to visit Rome and not indulge in its scrumptious gelati. Indeed the Italian passion for ice-cream has led to a multitude of unusual flavours – apple, fig, papaya, pinenut, white chocolate, profiterole, tiramasu, zabaglione … the choice is endless. At Fiocco di Neve (Via Maddalena 51), rice is added to many of the traditional flavours to provide crunch, while Gelateria della Palma (Via delle Copelle 78) boasts over a 100 flavours as well as mousses, frozen yoghurts and a variety of toppings – fresh fruit, nuts, sauces and whipped cream.

Rebuilding Rome

As Rome rapidly approaches its fourth millennium, perhaps more than ever before it is the place to contemplate the passage of time. In no other city are the accumulated layers of history so evident as in Rome, and the months leading up to 2000 (known as Il Giubileo in Italian) have provided the perfect opportunity to give Rome a facelift.

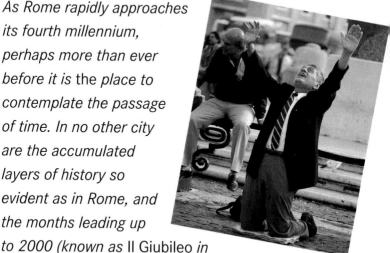

The changing face of Rome

Once again Rome is at the leading edge of a centuries-old problem – how to modernise and improve without destroying its past. Julius Caesar (101–44 BC) was the first in Rome to introduce a major building programme to build a city fit for an empire, while Emperor Augustus (27 BC–AD 14) boasted that he had found the city made of brick and left it made of marble. Rome's great Baroque city planner, **Pope Sixtus V's** main contribution to city planning was to improve communications for pilgrims, with a vast network of streets linking all the city gates. More recently, **Mussolini's** delusions of imperial grandeur led to a spate of building which ploughed mercilessly through sites of ancient Rome.

Millennium mania

This time round **Francesco Rutelli**, Mayor of Rome, has had the unenviable task of co-ordinating the Millennium rebuilding projects, and of pacifying ceaseless opposition from archaeologists who feared that every new road, underpass or car park, intended to ease nightmarish traffic problems, would destroy the heritage of the city. Various projects have had to be abandoned, including the construction of Metro Line C, the underpass beneath Castel Sant' Angelo near the Vatican, and a railway line linking central Rome to its second airport at Ciampino. But with such plans as a gigantic car park and hotel complex next to the Vatican still progressing, **Alberto Ronchey**, former Minister of Culture has accused Signor Rutelli of 'bowing to the Vatican's demands' and making Rome a 'supermarket for the soul'.

A Holy Year

As over 30 million pilgrims and visitors flood to Rome, the Millennium will be, above all, a religious celebration – a Holy Year. By then, the city will no longer be a gigantic building site with half its sights smothered in scaffolding. The frenzy of restoration projects should finally be complete and the Eternal City returned once more to its former glory.

Via Veneto and Quirinale

Noble Monte Quirinale – the highest of Rome's 'Seven Hills' – studded with magnificent Baroque palaces, churches and fountains, became the residence of the kings of Italy in 1870, and is home today to her head of state, the President of the Republic of Italy. Nearby, once-glitzy Via Veneto serves as a faded reminder of the city's more recent heyday in the 1950s when Rome's Cinecittà film studios were Europe's answer to Hollywood.

VIA VENETO AND QUIRINALE

via Veneto and Quirinale

*Getting there: **Metro:** Metro A has stops at Termini, Piazza della Repubblica (Repubblica) and Piazza Barberini (Barberini). **Bus:** Buses No. 52, 53, 56, 58, 60, 61, 62, 71, 95, 116 and 492 go up Via del Tritone to Piazza Barberini. Nos. 52, 53, 56, 58, 95 and 116 continue up Via Veneto while Nos. 62 and 492 go on to Piazza della Repubblica. For the Museo Nazionale Romano take any bus to Termini train station. For Santa Maria Maggiore, hop on Nos. 4, 9, 14, 16, 70, 71, 75 or 714. No buses go up Via del Quirinale to the top of Quirinal Hill so take Nos. 64, 70, 170 or 164 along Via Nazionale to Via IV Novembre then walk up Via XXIV Maggio to Piazza del Quirinale or Via delle Quatro Fontane. Electric minibus 117 bisects Via Nazionale, Quirinal Hill and Via del Tritone en route for the Spanish Steps.*

① *Fontana di Trevi*

Toss a coin over your shoulder into Rome's largest and most spectacular fountain to ensure your return to the Eternal City! Bring your camera too, as the irresistible confection of tritons, sea horses, rock pools and waves, wedged into a pocket-sized *piazzetta*, makes the Trevi Fountain one of Rome's most photogenic spectacles. **Page 94**

② *Count the bees*

Great fun for children! The bee is the emblem of Rome's great Barberini family and can be seen throughout this district on fountains, on buildings, in paintings ... in fact, everywhere! **Page 98**

③ *Museo Nazionale Romano*

Don't hold your breath, as this museum has been closed for restoration for decades! However, it *is* finally due to reopen prior to the Millennium, and promises to be worth the wait since it contains one of the largest and most important collections of Classical Roman art in the world. **Page 96**

④ *Pasta Museum*

A visit to the Museo Nazionale delle Paste Alimentari – one of Rome's newest museums with an intriguing motto 'If flour is silver, semolina is gold' – will tell you everything you ever needed to know about Italy's favourite dish, and a lot more besides. An absolute must for food lovers! **Page 94**

⑤ *Santa Maria Maggiore*

The largest of Rome's 80 churches dedicated to the Virgin, and arguably the most beautiful, Santa Maria Maggiore is especially famed for its blend of architectural styles, its shimmering mosaics and its sumptuous papal chapels, extravagant even by Baroque standards. **Page 102**

⑥ *La Dolce Vita*

Sit in a pavement café on Via Veneto, close your eyes and imagine the hedonistic Rome of the 60s with its sexy movie stars and flash-popping paparazzi, its wild nightlife and its grand hotels, all recorded for posterity by Rome's leading moviemaker, Federico Fellini in his classic film *La Dolce Vita*. **Page 103**

⑦ *Castor and Pollux*

Atop Quirinal Hill with its panoramic views over the city, the two giant statues of Castor and Pollux – popularly known as the 'horse tamers' – have given Piazza del Quirinale its nickname *Monte Cavallo* or 'Horse Hill'. **Page 98**

Tourist information

The main Tourism Agency of Rome (*Azienda di Promozione Turistica di Roma*, also called the *EPT* or *Ente Provinciale per il Turismo di Roma*) is based at *Via Parigi 5* (*tel: (06) 48899253/255*; *open Mon–Sat, 0815–1915*). They will also help with accommodation. Another EPT branch can be found at the main Termini railway station (*tel: (06) 4824078*), although it tends to be more crowded.

There are also small 'Informa Roma' tourist information kiosks in the ticket hall of Termini station (*tel: (06) 48906300*) and on Via Nazionale just outside the Palazzo Esposizioni (*tel: (06) 47824525, both open daily 0900–1800*).

93

Fontana dell' Aqua Felice
('Fountain of the Happy Water' or 'Moses Fountain')

Piazza San Bernardo.

This vast fountain with its three elegant arches designed by Domenico Fontana, was the first of the big post-Renaissance *mostra* or 'show' fountains commissioned by popes to celebrate the reopening of the city's ancient aqueducts. It is popularly named after the ill-proportioned, larger-than-life central figure of **Moses** by sculptor Prospero Bresciano, inspired by Michelangelo's giant sculpture. Following the fountain's unveiling in 1586, his amateurish work soon made him a laughing stock. He died soon after of a broken heart.

Fontana di Trevi
(Trevi Fountain)

Piazza di Trevi.

The Trevi Fountain is one of Rome's best-loved sights – an over-the-top, Baroque extravaganza of ancient sea gods and gushing water out of all proportion to the tiny piazza, at the meeting point of *tre vie* (three streets). It marks the site of one of Rome's earliest fountains, and was constructed in 1732–62 as a *mostra* (show), following the ancient Roman custom of decorating the spot where water emerged with a great fountain. The Trevi water – from the Acqua Vergine (*see page 117*) – is reputedly Rome's sweetest; however, the rite of drinking it to assure your return to the Eternal City has been superseded by **the tossing-in of a coin**. The coins get scooped out every week, supposedly for charity.

The fountain was designed by Nicola Salvi, using a wall of Palazzo Poli as a backdrop. Entire houses had to be torn down to make room for the monumental construction, which followed the popular marine mythology of the age: a massive figure of **Neptune** (framed by a triumphal arch) riding a sea-shell drawn by conch-blowing tritons and seahorses splashing their way out of the fountain – the rearing steed symbolising the ocean in turmoil and the calm one its tranquillity. Two figures representing **Health** and **Abundance** look on from the side niches and the carved panels above depict the discovery of the Acqua Vergine in 19 BC, apparently revealed to Roman soldiers by a virgin.

" *I like this city. It is full of the sound of water, fountains everywhere, amazing and beautiful – big things full of marble – gods and animals, naked girls wrestling with horses and swans with tons of water cascading over them.* "

William Faulkner (1954)

The end result is so much like a stage-set that later architects added rows of seats from which to admire Rome's most sensational fountain. If, by day, you find it rather too crowded for enjoyment, return by night when spotlights play magically on the newly-cleaned marble and gushing water, making it one of the most delightful corners of Rome.

Museo Nazionale delle Pasta Alimentari (National Pasta Museum)

Piazza Scanderberg 117. Tel: (06) 6991119. Open daily 0930–1730. Admission: £££ (includes portable CD player with 30-min multilingual commentary).

Bored with picturesque palaces and rambling ruins? Then come to the world's only museum dedicated to pasta! Inside, 11 rooms of colourful *al dente* exhibits provide a crash course in the history of pasta from the thin mix of water and wheat used in Etruscan days to the gleaming modern machinery that churns out today's popular product. Rare manuscripts chronical milestones in **pasta history**, each region fashioning their own distinctive shapes, such as *vermicelli* in Naples and *tortellini* in Bologna (reputedly inspired by Venus's navel). The museum displays all shapes, sizes and colours of pasta from *amorini* (little cupids) to *ziti* (bridegrooms) with pasta sculptures, pasta paintings, pasta prints and some amusing photos of international personalities tucking into piping hot helpings of the nation's favourite dish.

Museo Nazionale Romano
(National Roman Museum)

Viale Enrico de Nicola 79. Tel: (06) 48903507. Open Tue–Sat 0900–1400;
Sun 0900–1300 (currently closed for restoration). Closed Mon. Admission: ££.

Here, one of the world's greatest collections of Classical Roman art is kept behind lock and key! For years the museum has been closed – awaiting restoration – but it is expected to reopen for the Millennium.

> " *Rome is the only European capital which each year must spend millions of pounds restoring ruins – restoring them at least to their state of ruin of 100 years ago!* "
>
> **British journalist George Armstrong**

If you are lucky enough to get inside, you will find a labyrinth of precious treasures: row upon row of priceless Classical statues lining fine cloisters built by **Michelangelo**, room after room of magnificent mosaics, stuccos, sarcophagi and frescoes in part of the great **Baths of Diocletian** (ancient Rome's largest public baths) and, most prized of all, the *Ludovisi Throne*, an original, highly decorative Greek sculpture from the fifth century BC, which Mussolini sold to Hitler in 1938. In Diocletian's time, a garden surrounded the baths. Still today the museum is fringed by cypress trees and pink and white oleanders which shade huge vases, mosaics and other archaeological fragments.

Palazzo Barberini – Galleria Nazionale d'Arte Antica (Barberini Palace – National Gallery of Ancient Art)

Via Barberini 18/Via Quattro Fontane 13. Tel: (06) 4824184, 4814591.
Open Tue–Sat 0900–1900, Sun 0900–1300 (last entry 30-mins before closing).
Closed Mon. Admission: £££.

The Barberini family's pontiff, Urban VIII, had Rome's top Baroque architects working on this enormous family home from 1625 until 1633. Its unusual layout – an oversized cream country villa with three imposing storeys of arcades, flanked by terracotta-coloured wings – was primarily designed by **Maderno**. After his death, it was finished by **Bernini** and **Borromini** who between them added such

Palazza Barberini

theatrical touches as a square and an oval spiral stairway and the imaginative *tromp l'oeil* side windows on the upper floor of the main (west) façade. Architectural rivals for decades, Bernini (financially backed for over 20 years by the Barberini family) believed Borromini 'had been sent to destroy architecture', while Borromini was eventually driven to suicide in 1667, claiming that Bernini stole all his ideas and designs.

Since it became state property in 1949, the Palazzo has housed one of the city's most important museums – the Galleria Nazionale d'Arte Antica – with a priceless collection of medieval, Baroque and Renaissance art occupying most of the palazzo's *piano nobile* (first floor), and 18th-century paintings on the floor above. Italian painting is well represented, with works by Lorenzo, Lippi, Lotto, Titian, Caravaggio, Reni and, most precious of all, Raphael's *La Fornarina* (thought to be a portrait of the baker's daughter and mistress with whom Raphael indulged in the pleasures of love to such an extent that it caused his death!). Look out also for foreign artists Metys and Poussin, and Holbein's famous portrait of England's *King Henry VIII*.

Be sure to see the Barberini apartments, with their effusively frescoed walls and period furnishings, and the palace's most important room – the *Gran Salon* – with its overwhelming ceiling by Pietro da Cortona (*The Triumph of Divine Providence*, 1633–9). It celebrates the virtues of Pope Urban VIII for whom it was painted (note the three bees swarming about the heavens taken from the Barberini coat of arms, very much in evidence throughout the palace) and is considered another of Rome's great Baroque masterpieces.

Piazza Barberini

Piazza Barberini.

Piazza Barberini is best known for its two famous Baroque fountains, constructed in honour of the great Florentine family after which the square is named. At the centre of the noisy, traffic-filled square, the **Fontana del Tritone (Triton Fountain)** was Bernini's earliest fountain. Created in 1637, it is a favourite of the Romans – a joyful marine god rises triumphantly out of the sea, kneeling on two scallop shells held aloft by entwined dolphins, and blowing a high jet of water out of a conch shell. Look more closely and you will notice the family's papal tiara, the keys of St Peter's and the distinctive Barberini coat of arms, with its three bees.

Why a bee as the Barberini emblem? Nobody knows for certain, but some say that in the early 17th century (when the Barberini name became important here) Rome was invaded

Triton Fountain

by swarms of bees. The second fountain in the square (on the corner of Via Veneto) is a modest Bernini work. Aptly named the **Fontana delle Api (Bee Fountain)**, its three giant bees sit on a giant scallop shell, sipping the trickling water flowing into the large basin beneath. The inscription on the shell dedicates the fountain once again to Pope Urban VIII, patriarch of the Barberini family.

Piazza del Quirinale

Piazza del Qurinale.

Lined with handsome palaces, adorned with ancient statues and cooled by a fountain, Piazza del Quirinale is the epitome of Roman elegance, affording a bird's-eye view of the city with the dome of St Peter's in the distance. Its centrepiece is two giant 5.5m equestrian statues of **Castor and Pollux**,

Imperial-era copies of Greek originals dating from the fifth century BC, restored by Sixtus V and transferred from the Baths of Constantine nearby. Two centuries later, Pius VI moved the figures apart to add an obelisk from the entrance to Augustus' mausoleum, and 40 years later Pius VII, not to be left out, added a splendid antique basin, formerly used as a water trough in the Forum when it was used for grazing cattle.

If you think the massive orange palace crowning the piazza seems familiar, look no further than your pocket – it's on the back of a L500 coin! Originally built as a summer residence for popes, and guarded by smartly-uniformed *Granatiere* (chosen for their height and good looks), Palazzo del Quirinale has housed Kings of Italy since 1870 and Presidents of Italy since 1947. Here too the new Republic was born in November 1848 when a revolutionary mob attacked the palace and captured the pope.

Beginning in 1574, most of the finest architects of the Counter-Reformation and Baroque periods had a hand in the construction of the palace, including Bernini who designed the Loggia of the Benedictions above the main entrance and the *manica lunga* (long sleeve) a long, narrow wing running a quarter of a kilometre along Via del Quirinale, making it one of the longest palaces in Italy. Inside is a veritable treasure trove of art ranging from Roman frescoes in the cellars to important paintings by Melozzo da Forli, Pietro da Cortona and others but sadly, for security reasons, the palace and gardens are rarely open to the public. *Tel: (06) 46991; open Sept–July on the second and fourth Sunday of each month 0800–1230.*

99

‘There are no Romans, only people from all parts of Italy who adopt Roman characteristics. ,,

20th-century Roman novelist, Alberto Moravia

Le Quattro Fontane
(The Four Fountains)

Via del Quirinale/Via delle Quattro Fontane.

In 1593 Rome's great Baroque city planner, Pope Sixtus V, commissioned fountains representing the Rivers Tiber and Nile and the goddesses Juno and Diana at the four corners of this important crossroads in 1593.

It was a typically Baroque concept to link major places of pilgrimage by carving straight streets through the hotchpotch of medieval lanes and alleyways, and positioning fountains and obelisks along them. From here, **three obelisks are visible** – those of the Pincio, Esquiline and Quirinal hills – emphasising the religious importance of this symbolic cross: Via del Quirinale led from the former papal summer palace (Palazzo del Quirinale, *see page 98*) to *Porta Pie* city gate (Door of the Faithful) while Via delle Quattro Fontane (an extension of Via Sistina) reached from Trinità dei Monti (*see page 115*) to Santa Maria Maggiore (*see page 102*). Thankfully, Sixtus died before he was able to implement his plan to demolish the Colosseum, which blocked the route from San Giovanni in Laterano to St Peter's!

Sant' Andrea al Quirinale

Via del Quirinale 29. Tel: (06) 48903187. Open 0800–1200, 1600–1900. Closed Tue. Admission: £.

Yet another Baroque *tour de force* by architectural genius Gianlorenzo Bernini. No expense was spared on this lavish church, commissioned in 1658 by the Jesuits, who believed the glory of heaven could best be demonstrated to the faithful by worldly opulence. The curvaceous **oval-shaped interior** is truly astonishing, bedecked in sumptuous pink marble, ornamental maritime motifs (a constant reminder of its patron saint, the fisherman St Andrew) and endearing stucco *putti* (cherubs) clustered around the gilded dome. Remove the altar and it could almost be a ballroom!

Santa Maria della Concezione – Convento dei Cappuccini
(Church of the Immaculate Conception – Capucin Convent)

Via Veneto 27. Open Fri–Wed 0900–1200, 1500–1800. Closed Thur. Admission: ££ (an obligatory 'donation').

> " *Rome reminds me of a man who lives by exhibiting to travellers his grandmother's corpse.* "
>
> **James Joyce**

Rome's most ghoulish chamber of horrors lies in the crypt of this otherwise unimpressive church – a bone-chilling *coemeterium* (cemetery) with five **subterranean chapels**, each grotesquely decorated with the bones and skulls of over 4,000 Capuchin monks, and with a number of full skeletons standing guard. It supposedly represents 'a joyous celebration of Death', and is not without artistic merit. However, it is not recommended for those of sensitive disposition or for young children!

The church was built in 1624 for Cardinal Antonio Barberini, brother of Urban VIII, a Capuchin friar whose humble **tombstone** set in the pavement before the main altar simply states *Hic jacet pulvis, cinis et nihil* (Here lies dust, ashes and nothing).

Santa Maria della Vittoria

Via XX Settembre 17. Open daily 0630–1200, 1630–1930. Admission: £.

Designed in 1646 for the Venetian Cardinal Cornaro, this is one of Rome's most richly decorated churches, whose interior was mostly executed by Bernini and pupils. Bernini was also a stage designer. In a stroke of theatrical mastery, he seated eight sculptures of Cornaro's family in recesses resembling theatre boxes in the **Cornaro chapel**. The subject of their attention and the church's greatest treasure is his remarkable **sculpture**, *The Ecstasy of St Teresa*, showing the saint pierced by the love of God. St Teresa's own account of her ecstasy was so loaded with ambiguous sexual imagery that the sculpture has attracted as much scorn as praise. One critic described it as 'quite the most unfit ornament to place in a Christian church' while writer Hyppolite Taine remarked 'through the transfigured, palpitating marble, we see the soul flooded with joy and rapture, shining like a lamp'.

Santa Maria Maggiore

Piazza di Santa Maria Maggiore. Tel: (06) 483195. Open daily 0700–1900.
Admission: £.

Santa Maria Maggiore has many claims to fame: it is the finest example of an early Christian basilica, the only church where Mass has been celebrated every day since the 5th century, one of Rome's four great patriarchal basilicas (with St Peter's, San Giovanni in Laterano and San Paolo fuori le Mura) and a major point of pilgrimage.

Architectural wonder

Of all Roman basilicas, Santa Maria Maggiore has the most successful blend of architectural styles. The lofty triple nave, enhanced by 40 ancient columns, are part of the original fifth-century building. The marble-decorated pavement and bell-tower (the tallest in Rome) are medieval, the flat coffered ceiling is Renaissance (supposedly gilded in the first gold brought back from the Americas), whilst the twin domes, façades and two papal chapels are Baroque.

The Capella Sistina, embellished with gilt and precious stones ransacked from other ancient buildings, was designed for Sixtus V. Paul V's larger, flamboyantly bejewelled Capella Paolina was constructed to house a highly revered Madonna and Child icon, said to be painted by St Luke. It contains a relief by Maderno showing Pope Liberius planning the original basilica, following a dream in which

the Virgin instructed him to build a church on the spot where snow would fall the next morning, 5 August 352 AD. The anniversary of this miracle is commemorated annually at the feast of the Madonna della Neve (Our Lady of the Snow), when thousands of white petals are released from the roof of the church.

Near the main altar, an over-sized statue of Pope Pius IX kneels before the most prized relic – five pieces of wood bound with iron, said to be pieces of Christ's crib from Bethlehem, on view only on the 25th of every month.

Miraculous mosaics

The church's interior beauty stems mainly from its gleaming mosaics: the 36 scenes from the Old Testament (in the nave) which date from the fifth century, the gold-tinged Byzantine-style scenes of the *Annunciation* and the *Infancy of Christ* (in the altar's triumphal arch) and, most spectacular of all, the 13th-century mosaics by Franciscan monk Jacopo Torriti (in the apse) depicting Mary being crowned *Queen of Heaven* by Christ – considered by many the pinnacle of Rome's mosaic tradition.

Via Veneto

Thanks to Federico Fellini, Rome's greatest moviemaker, the most photographed street in Rome is famous worldwide as the glamorous backdrop for such classic films as *Roma* and *La Dolce Vita* (*see pages 106–107*). Via Veneto has been a fun-loving area since Julius Caesar's time. But Fellini captured on celluloid the street's heyday of the 1950s and 60s, when its sophisticated *belle epoque* hotels and chic pavement cafés were frequented by such Hollywood greats as Sophia Loren, Frank Sinatra, Ava Gardner, Ingrid Bergman, Errol Flynn, Anthony Quinn, Orson Wells, Sean Connery, Humphrey Bogart, Kirk Douglas, Richard Burton, Liz Taylor …

103

66 *This church is a gem of beauty which Time and the Tiber and the vandals of the 16th and 17th centuries have been unable to rob of its glory.* 99

O Potter, *The Colour*

Unfortunately, the hedonistic days of *la dolce vita* are no longer so apparent, the film stars largely replaced by tourists. Yet Via Veneto still has an undeniable magic. Strolling down its lazy, tree-lined curve from Porta Pinciana to Piazza Barberini, past some of the city's most luxurious hotels and exclusive boutiques, it is easy to imagine you are on a living film set.

Cafés and restaurants

Although Via Veneto is no longer the street of star-studded dreams of the 50s and 60s, it remains a fashionable district with luxury as the keynote and more than its fair share of exclusive (£££) restaurants, notably George's *(*Via Marche 7, tel: (06) 42084575*) with its cut glass, crisp white linens and al fresco dining;* Le Sans Souci *(*Via Sicilia 20, tel: (06) 4821814*) serving French and Italian cuisine in a smart black-and-gold interior and, most famous of all, the lavish* belle epoque *dining room of* Hotel Excelsior *(*Via Veneto 125, tel: (06) 4708*) with its gilt, drapes, marble and mirrors, frequented by all the stars of* la dolce vita.

Est! Est! Est!

Via Amedeo 4a. Tel: (06) 4881107. £. Closed Mon and Aug. One of Rome's oldest pizzerias (named after a local wine) with three noisy, fun dining rooms serving cheap, cheerful pizza and pasta near Termini station.

Gargani

Via Lombardia 15/17. Tel: (06) 4740865. ££. Closed Sun. One of many delicatessens that double up as restaurants at lunchtime. Simply point to a selection of *antipasti*, take a seat on the shady terrace and await your meal.

Al Picchio

Via del Lavatore 40. Tel: (06) 6789926. £. Closed Sun. Of the many touristic restaurants around the Trevi fountain, this one, with its attentive service and simple, nourishing portions of pasta, meat and vegetables, is excellent value.

Il Pomodorino

Via Campania 45/e. Tel: (06) 42011356. £. Closed Sat lunch. Off the beaten track near Villa Borghese, this huge pizzeria is especially busy at weekends, frequented by a young and lively crowd keen to try the home-made pasta, the home-baked bread and the crisp pizzas cooked in vast wood-fired ovens.

Il Posto Accanto

Via del Boschetto 36a. Tel: (06) 4743002. ££–£££. Closed Sat lunch, Sun and Aug. Tiny, sophisticated yet romantic, this family-run restaurant offers a simple menu of familiar cuisine, including one of the best *tiramasù* in Rome.

Shopping

Alexia
Via Nazionale 75u/76/77/78. One of Rome's largest selections of leather goods, handbags and luggage at reasonable prices.

L'Antico Forno
Via delle Muratte 8/Piazza Trevi. This delicatessen is perfectly positioned for a picnic on the steps of the Trevi Fountain.

Fiorucci
Via Nazionale 236. Hip fashions at affordable prices for young, image-conscious Italians.

Manufattura Guanti
Via Nazionale 183. Look out for this tiny, old-fashioned shop, lined with boxes and drawers containing traditional leather gloves, bags, belts and wallets.

Museum Shop
Via Nazionale 185. A good fun souvenir shop stocking brightly painted espresso cups, tasteful 'Rome' T-shirts, art pens and Colosseum soaps and other innovative gift ideas.

Rizzoli
Largo Chigi 15. Rome's largest bookshop.

Nightlife

The Quirinale has been a fun-loving area ever since it belonged to Julius Caesar. Some of today's most popular haunts include **Harry's Bar** (*Via Veneto 150*), one of the cult spots of the Via Veneto and *la dolce vita* and **Planet Hollywood** (*Via del Tritone 118*) eternally popular, with happy hour every weekday from 1600–2000. **Café Renault** (*Via Nazionale 183/b*), with its trendy chrome interior and giant video screens has its own Renault Espace to shuttle customers to and from the bar from Piazza Venezia and Piazza della Repubblica, and walking into the wild **Bayside Café** (*Via Sardegna 61/63*) is like stepping off a plane into the Caribbean with its bright blue sea-and-sailing-boat décor and its exotic cocktails served by waiters in jazzy Hawaiian shirts. Nearby, piano bar and nightclub **Jackie O'** (*Via Boncampagni 11*), one of *the* venues of Via Veneto in its heyday, still appeals to an older, well-heeled clientele.

Celebrities

During the golden era of la dolce vita, *the cafés of Via Veneto were the places to spot celebrities, stars and socialites where cafés such as Doney's (* No. 145 *) and the Café de Paris (* No. 90 *) were immortalised by Richard Burton and Liz Taylor, Ingrid Bergman, Frank Sinatra and Ava Gardner to name but a few. Still today Romans mix business with pleasure in the pavement cafés of this nostalgic street.*

Hollywood on the Tiber

On 29 January 1936, megalomaniac Benito Mussolini laid the foundation stone of Cinecittà film studios, designed to produce propaganda for his Fascist regime. Little did he know that it was to become the Hollywood of Europe in the glorious 1950s and 60s, producing countless silver screen classics such as Ben Hur, Quo Vadis? Helen of Troy, *and* Cleopatra, *and enabling many of the great Italian film directors to make their debut.*

La Dolce Vita

The best-known Italian film produced during this golden era was *La Dolce Vita*, in which Italy's great Federico Fellini recorded for posterity this post-war age of decadence and exhibitionism, which revolved around the glitzy haunts of the Via Veneto and their international film star patrons, in constant flight from reporters and photographers. He reproduced some of their more capricious activities on celluloid – including the notorious scene when Anita Ekberg, one of the sexiest actresses of the time, took a late-night dip in the **Fontana di Trevi** (*pictured opposite*). The celebrated fountain also featured in his *Three Coins in the Fountain.*

La Dolce Vita made a huge impact internationally, winning the Palme d'Or at the 1960 Cannes film festival, and making Fellini and Rome inseparable in the annals of cinema. Still today, the film is very much with us: its title has entered our everyday vocabulary as the definition of the pursuit of frivolous pleasures, and even the name of the photo-journalist in the film, **Paparazzo**, is now used to refer to the relentless tabloid photographers who strive to get celebrity snapshots at all costs.

Contemporary cinema

Unfortunately the high life portrayed in Fellini's *La Dolce Vita* faded long ago and **Cinecittà** works at only half the capacity it did at its peak 40 years ago. It is now mostly used for making advertisements and television series, yet it still occasionally makes its mark on box-offices worldwide with such international blockbusters as *The Godfather III*, *The Name of the Rose*, *The Last Emperor* and *The English Patient*. Its legendary studios (southeast of the city centre) are open to visitors, but do phone ahead for an appointment. *Via Tuscolana 1055, tel: (06) 722931, take Metro A to Cinecittà.*

Il Tridente

Tourists are drawn as if by a magnet to 'Il Tridente' – three streets diverging from Piazza del Popolo like the prongs of a trident – for this is Rome's most fashionable shopping district, offering an A to Z of fashion and design from Armani to Zegna, interwoven with some of the most memorable and popular sights of Rome.

Getting there: **Metro:** *Metro A has stops at both the Piazza di Spagna and Flaminio (Piazza del Popolo).*
Bus: *Electric minibus 117 loops around a large part of Il Tridente, travelling along the Corso, Via del Babuino and through both Piazza di Spagna and Piazza del Popolo every 15 minutes. Other useful buses include Nos. 628 and 926 along Via Ripetta and Nos. 81, 115, 492 and 628 along the Corso. Additionally, there is a major bus terminal (Nos. 52, 53, 58, 61, 71, 85 and 160) near Via Condotti at Piazza di San Silvestro.*

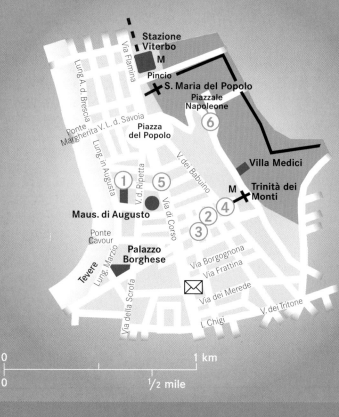

IL TRIDENTE

① An ancient 'Altar of Peace'

After such formidable sights as the Colosseum and the Forum, a simple altar may not sound all that inspiring, but this masterpiece of Roman sculpture combining legend, history and religion is one of the great treasures of Imperial Rome, lost for centuries but painstakingly reconstructed in the 1930s by Mussolini. **Page 112**

② Join the rich and famous

Enjoy a coffee-break or an early evening glass of prosecco in Caffè Greco, an old-style café frequented over the centuries by such illustrious visitors as Rubens, Berlioz, Baudelaire, Goethe, Wagner, Liszt, Stendhal, Thackeray, Byron, Keats and Shelley. **Page 118**

③ Shop 'till you drop

Go home with a suitcase full of designer fashions from Rome's most famous shopping streets, centred around Via Condotti. Although fashion predominates, there are wonderful galleries, delicatessens and antiques shops to explore too. **Page 119**

④ Scale the Spanish Steps

The Scalinata di Trinità dei Monti (Spanish Steps) are at the top of many visitors' 'must-see' list. Ideally located at the heart of the city's fashion district, the steps are an ideal place to lounge around and rest your weary feet after all that shopping. **Page 115**

⑤ When in Rome ...

... Do as the Romans, and take part in one of their favourite pastimes, the late afternoon *passeggio*. Just dress up in your most fashionable outfit and promenade up and down the life-sized catwalk of the Corso or the Via Condotti along with half the population of the city, allegedly window-shopping but really checking out what everyone else is wearing. **Pages 117 and 118**

⑥ Scenic sunsets

Climb Pincio hill for one of the best panoramas in Rome. From here, the 'trident' of streets radiating out of Piazza del Popolo becomes clear, and there is an exceptional view of the many domes piercing the skyline from Santa Maria del Popolo (the oldest) to St Peter's (the largest) at the Vatican – particularly stunning when bathed in golden light at sunset. **Page 116**

Tip

As this is your day for shopping and self-indulgence, check shop opening times (see page 187) and don't pick Sunday or Monday morning, when most shops are closed.

111

Tourist information

There are no tourist information booths in this district. The nearest one is just off the Corso, at Largo Carlo Goldoni, *open daily 0900–1800 (tel: (06) 68136061).*

Ara Pacis Augustae

*Via di Ripetta – Lungotevere in Augusta. Open Tue, Wed, Fri and Sat
0900–1900; Thur 0900–1800; Sun 0900–1300; Closed Mon. Admission: ₤₤.*

The 'Altar of Peace' is one of the great treasures of ancient
Rome, commissioned by the Senate in 13 BC to celebrate

Augustus' victorious campaigns
in Spain and Gaul. For many
centuries it was lost and it was
only in the 1930s, to celebrate
the 2,000th anniversary of
Augustus' inauguration as
Emperor – during Mussolini's
attempts to link his regime to
imperial Rome – that its many
fragments were eventually
reassembled. Sadly, however, it
is encased in an ugly Fascist
concrete-and-glass building.

The altar is contained in a magnificent four-sided marble
enclosure smothered with some of the most beautiful
carvings in Rome, their delicately sculpted acanthus-leaf
patterns and stylised flowers influenced by the lyrical lines
of Hellenistic art. The eastern panel portrays the triumphal
parade to celebrate Augustus' return from battle to a
hero's welcome in 43 BC, and the consecration of the altar.
Augustus (taller than the other figures) leads the procession
of dignitaries, together with
four *flamine* (unusually-
hatted priests responsible
for lighting Rome's
ceremonial fires) and the
official sacrificer (the man
with an axe). A useful
booklet on sale will put
names to the other faces.

" *Shall I ever forget the sensations I
experienced, upon slowly descending the
hills, and crossing the bridge over the
Tyber, when I entered an avenue between
terraces and ornamented gates of villas,
which leads to the Porto del Popolo and
beheld the square, the domes, the
obelisk: the long perspective of streets
and palaces opening beyond, all glowing
with the vivid red of sun-set?* **"**

**William Beckford, traveller, collector
and English Member of Parliament,** *The
Grand Tour of William Beckford***, 1896**

Piazza del Popolo

One of the grandest squares in Rome, for centuries Piazza del Popolo was the main entrance to Rome for pilgrims from the north. Its most striking feature is the ancient obelisk, the oldest in Rome, brought here in around 10 BC by Augustus after the conquest of Egypt. It once decorated the Circus Maximus, where it was used as a turning point during chariot races. Today it is glorified by fountains and guarded by carved lions. In later years, the square became the papacy's favourite place for executions. The paving was allegedly paid for by taxes levied on prostitutes!

The Piazza's greatest monument is undoubtedly **Santa Maria del Popolo** (*open Mon–Sat 0700–1330, 1600–1900; Sun 0730–1930; admission: £*), tucked into the old city walls. The church was constructed in 1472 over a pre-existing 11th-century chapel, originally built on top of Nero's tomb to chase away his ghost, which supposedly

haunted the area. Its richly decorated interior is crammed with Renaissance and Baroque art treasures – notably the apse (designed by Bramante with frescoes by Pinturicchio), the Chigi Chapel (designed by Raphael but completed by Bernini) and two Caravaggio masterpieces (*The Conversion of St Paul* and *Crucifixion of St Peter*) in the chapel just left of the apse.

113

Neighbouring the church, the monumental triple-arched **Porta del Popolo** gateway was designed by Michelangelo in the 16th century. In the 17th century Cardinal Gastaldi added two domed churches – **Santa Maria dei Miracoli** (*open daily 0800–1300, 1700–1900; admission: £*) and **Santa Maria in Montesanto** (*open daily Apr–Oct 1700–2000; Nov–Mar 1600–1900; admission: £*) – which at first glimpse appear identical, but actually one is round and the other elliptical. In 1814, Napoleon instructed Valadier to give the square the elegant oval shape we see today.

Piazza di Spagna

This colourful and spacious 'Spanish Square' of elegant russet, ochre, salmon- and apricot-coloured palazzi, *takes its name from the stolid Palazzo di Spagna in the south-west corner, built in the 17th century as the Spanish Embassy to the Holy See. It has long been one of Rome's most famous and popular spots – best known for its so-called 'Spanish Steps'.*

Famous residents

In the 18th century, Piazza di Spagna became the favourite quarter of Rome for illustrious artists and Grand Tourists (*see pages 120–121*) from all over Europe – many of whom made it their home, including Balzac, Goethe, Wagner, Liszt, Rubens, Elizabeth Browning, Berlioz, Byron, Tennyson, Shelley and so many English milords that locals nicknamed the district *il ghetto de l'inglese* (the English Ghetto). Its most famous resident was John Keats, who died in the pink house at the foot of the Spanish Steps in February 1821, aged only 25. Since 1909 the Casa di Keats has been open to the public as a memorial to this great English Romantic poet and his compatriots Percy Bysshe Shelley and Lord Byron. The rooms which Keats occupied on the first floor have been preserved, and contain a collection of

manuscripts, paintings, documents and memorabilia, including Keats' rather gruesome death mask plus a lock of his hair, and an extensive specialist library – one of the finest dedicated to Romanticism in Europe.

Piazza di Spagna 26. Open Mon–Fri 0900–1300, 1500–1800; Oct–Mar 1430–1730; also Sat in summer 1100–1400, 1500–1800; admission: ££; www.demon.co.uk/heritage/Keats.House.Rome.

The Spanish Steps

The Scalinata di Trinità dei Monti is the crowning glory of the piazza – an elegantly cascading Rococo stairway of golden stone financed by the French, designed by an Italian, but commonly known as the 'Spanish Steps'! A tourist honeypot, popular meeting point for lovers and shoppers, and favourite hangout for youths (especially since the opening of a McDonald's nearby), the 137 steps are crowded day and night, as people while away the hours chatting and watching the rest of Rome rush by at their feet. It is undoubtedly one of the best places to people-watch or to while away some sunny hours writing postcards. At the foot of the steps, there is a charming fountain in the shape of a half-sunken barge (*La Barcaccia*, 1629), wittily designed by Bernini's father Pietro to solve the problem of the low water level of the ancient aqueduct Acqua Vergine, which originally fed the Pantheon and many of the fountains and baths of ancient Rome. It is said that his inspiration for the fountain was a massive flooding of the Tiber on Christmas Day in 1598, which stranded a similar barge on top of Pincio hill!

" *I have seen the ruins of Rome, the Vatican, St Peter's, and all the miracles of ancient and modern art contained in that majestic city. The impression of it exceeds anything I have ever experienced in my travels.* "
Letter from Percy Bysshe Shelley to Thomas Love Peacock, December 1818

At the summit of the Spanish Steps, twin-towered Trinità dei Monti (*open daily 1000–1230, 1600–1800; admission: £*) is Rome's most photographed church. Inside, the colourful frescoes of the transept by Raphael's star pupil Giulio Romano and the two fine paintings by Michelangelo's prodigy, Daniele da Volterra (*Descent from the Cross and The Assumption*) are worth a glimpse, but the main reason to visit the church is to admire the stupendous views over the rooftops of Rome from the entrance.

Pincio

Pincio is one of the oldest gardens in Rome. The first known gardens here date from the first century BC, when Monte Pincio was known as Collis Hortulorum (the hill of gardens) and the finest gardens belonged to the villa of Lucullus, the general and epicure who, having conquered Northern Anatolia, brought the first cherry trees to Europe among other war trophies.

Today's park takes its name from a famous fourth-century garden, owned by the Pinci family. Its present-day layout, adjoining the gardens of Villa Borghese, was designed by Valadier in 1814, and instantly became one of the city's most popular parks with its broad shaded avenues of umbrella pines, palm trees and evergreen oaks ideally suited to Roman high society's fashionable practice of 'promenading'. The garden is best reached either along **Viale Trinità dei Monti** at the top of the Spanish Steps or by zig/zagging up steps out of **Piazza del Popolo**. Its maze of pathways are edged with busts of famous Italians and an unusual water clock on **Viale dell' Orlogio**, one of Rome's quirkier fountains. But Pincio is best known for the magical views from the terrace at **Piazzale Napoleone** – *the* place to watch the sun set over the city, with the dome of St Peter's silhouetted in gold.

Via Condotti

Despite its humble name (referring to the underground pipes carrying water from the Acqua Vergine, *see page 94*), this is the most glamorous street in Rome, boasting the most prestigious names in Italian fashion – Gucci, Bulgari, Ferragamo, MaxMara, Valentino … a veritable window-shopper's paradise (*see page 119*)!

Villa Medici

Accademia di Francia a Roma, Viale della Trinità dei Monti 1. Gardens open Sun am in spring and autumn, otherwise variable. Admission: ££.

Henry James described the gardens of the Villa Medici as 'perhaps the most enchanting place in Rome . . . possessed of an incredible, impossible charm' with their hedged walks, fountains, secret gardens, arbours and alcoves decorated with statues all in true Renaissance style. Like many Roman villas of the 16th century, the house has a severe, unadorned façade, but its garden side is smothered in ornately sculpted decoration.

In 1804 Napoleon purchased the villa from the Medici family to house the **French Academy** and still today students come here to study fine arts, literature and music, hoping to follow in the footsteps of such past academicians as composers Berlioz and Debussy and painters Fragonard, Boucher and Ingres. The students stage frequent exhibitions and recitals, and the main concerts of the city's most important summer festival – **RomaEuropa** – are performed in the grounds.

The terrace outside Villa Medici affords a sweeping panorama of the city's skyscape. The round fountain here contains a cannonball. Legend has it that it was shot from Castel Sant' Angelo by Queen Christina of Sweden, a lover of practical jokes, to awaken Cardinal Ferdinando de' Medici in order to invite him on a hunting trip!

" *The Pincio Gardens are not sunken like the Tuileries Gardens, they dominate 80 or 100 feet of the Tiber and the surrounding countryside. The view from them is superb. In winter, at about two o'clock, one often sees the young ladies of Rome getting out of their carriages and walking on foot; it is their Bois de Boulogne.* "

Stendhal, *Promenades dans Rome*

Restaurants and cafés

Dal Bolognese
Piazza del Popolo 1/2. Tel: (06) 3611426. £££. Closed Mon and part of Aug. A 'see-and-be-seen' restaurant, with reliable Bolognese cuisine served by white-frocked waiters.

Ciampini
Viale Trinità dei Monti. Tel: (06) 6785678. ££. The location of this café is more memorable than the food, with its sweeping views over the rooftops of Rome. Good for a light lunch.

Margutta Vegetariano
Via Margutta 118. Tel: (06) 32650577. ££. Want a change from pizza and pasta? You will be spoilt for choice with the unusual dishes at this, Rome's top vegetarian restaurant.

Nino's
Via Borgognona 11. Tel: (06) 6786752. ££–£££. Closed Sun and August. This popular, well-situated Tuscan trattoria near the Spanish Steps attracts the beautiful people of Rome. Try the *crostini toscani* to start followed by *bistecca alla fiorentina*.

Afternoon tea

When laden down with all your shopping, you are well placed here to rest awhile in of the district's many famous cafés. Choose between arch-rivals Caffè Rosati and Canova on Piazza del Popolo, traditional Caffè Grecco (Via Condotti 86), once a favourite meeting place for foreign artists and writers on the Grand Tour (see page 120–121) or Babington's Tea Rooms (Piazza di Spagna 23), little changed since it was opened in 1896 by two Englishwomen to serve homesick British tourists tea and scones.

Shopping

This is undoubtedly Rome's most fashionable district. Nowhere is the Italian flair for display more striking than in the haute couture boutiques and the stylish customers of Via Condotti and its surrounding grid of streets. Virtually every top Italian designer has an outlet here and many a happy hour can be spent gazing longingly at their inspirational window displays.

For starters, check out *Gucci*, *Valentino*, *Armani*, *Ferragamo*, *Buccellati* and *Battistoni* in Via Condotti; *Fendi*, *Ferre* and *Laura Biagotti* in Via Borgognona; *Krizia*, *Dolce e Gabbana* and *Raphael Salato* in Piazza di Spagna; *Versace*, *Moschino*, *Cucci* and *Ungaro* in Via Bocca di Leone. Accompany your new outfit with jewellery, either from *Pettocchi* (Piazza di Spagna), jewellers to Italy's former royal family, or the city's most splendid jewellery shop, *Bulgari* (Via Condotti).

Other noteworthy streets in the area include Via del Croce for sophisticated food stores, Via Babuino for antiques and Via Margutta for art galleries. In spring and autumn an outdoor art exhibition runs the length of the street.

Alinari

Via Alibert 16a. Hidden in a back street, this easily missed shop contains striking prints and old photographs of Rome.

Artistica

Via Babuino 24. If the beauty of Rome inspires you to commit its sights to canvas, you'll find everything you require in this small shop of artists' supplies.

Balloon

Piazza di Spagna 35. Affordable fashions in an unaffordable district.

C.U.C.I.N.A.

Via Babuino 118a. The ultimate in practical kitchen design. Come here for your pasta pan, your ravioli maker and your spaghetti servers!

DKNY

Via Frattina 44/45. Enter onto the catwalk in this futuristic, monochromatic shop with its latest trendy creations both visible on the peg and on massive video screens.

Discount dell' Alta Moda

Via Gesu e Maria 16. Remainders of last year's collections and sample pieces by internationally renowned designers at irresistible prices.

Enoteca Buccone

Via di Ripetta 19. A popular *vinicoli* (liqueur store) with bottles stacked from floor to ceiling, including the very best of local wines.

Sorelle Fontana

Salita di San Sebastianello 4–5. A veritable institution, the Fontana sisters have been clothing Rome's best-dressed women ever since its heyday in the *dolce vita* of the 1950s and 1960s.

Touring Club Italiana

Via Babuino 19. An excellent selection of coffee-table books on Rome, and polyglot travel guides and maps for all the regions of Italy.

The Grand Tour

Tourists are nothing new to Rome. Over the centuries, countless visitors have succumbed to the city's charms, often staying for lengthy periods or even taking up residence. In the 18th century it became fashionable for any well-to-do young gentleman – and occasionally young ladies too – to set out with a tutor or friend for a one- or two-year 'Grand Tour' of the continent, taking in the most famous cities, sights and artworks and culminating in a visit to Rome.

Travellers' tales

Their travels were often fraught with problems: **Casanova** was sexually assaulted by a policeman; **Joseph Addison** fell into the harbour on arrival at Calais; **Petrarch** was seriously injured by a horse, and **Tennyson** turned back at

◗ *Via Appia*

Florence, on discovering he could not buy his favourite brand of tobacco. However, their struggles were richly rewarded, as the treasures of Rome became the creative inspiration for countless writers, artists, architects and composers.

Reactions to Rome

Liszt, **Poussin** and **Nietzsche** produced their best works here; **Edward Gibbon** found inspiration for his classic *Decline and Fall of the Roman Empire* whilst musing amidst the ruins of the Capitol; **Lady Knight** wrote in her diaries (entitled *The Grand Tour*, 1728) 'We have been ten days in Rome and already have seen enough of it to make us think it the finest city in the world'; **Robert Adam**, 'equipped with all things needful to measure the dimensions of the antiquities', returned to England with a taste for Neoclassical design that led to one of the most prolific and brilliant periods of English architecture, and Goethe, like so many fellow Grand Tourists, found his visit to the 'First City of the world … guide and education to last a lifetime'.

Ruins of Circus Maxentius, Via Appia

The Grand Tour remained popular right through to the 19th century, but tourist trends gradually started to change. In 1864, **Thomas Cook** organised the first ever group 'package' tour from London, with pre-booked travel, accommodation, food and entertainment for 50 people, heralding the new era of mass tourism which still pervades the city today.

Trastevere

No-one should miss this atmospheric neighbourhood, long known as Rome's 'bohemian' district. By day, its patchwork of tight-knit streets strung with washing lines, its tumbledown houses and sun-bleached piazzete with their galleries and craft shops, appear sleepy. But by night, this is where Rome's heart beats the loudest, as Romans come flocking to Trastevere's popular pizzerias and trendy bars.

TRASTEVERE

Getting there: **By bus:** *Most bus routes in this district go along Viale di Trastevere, including No. 75 from Termini or No.170 from Piazza Venezia. From the Vatican take No. 23 or No. 280 along Lungotevere. Only one bus goes up Gianicolo Hill – No. 870 starting in Via Paola on the west bank of the river, although Nos. 44 and 75 will take you from Piazza Venezia to a suitably high point from which to start your walk.* **By tram:** *Tram No. 8 goes from Largo Torre Argentina to Piazza Sonnino and Viale Trastevere. Tram No. 30 circles the town from Villa Borghese, concluding at Piazzale Ostiense – just a short walk across the river to Trastevere.*

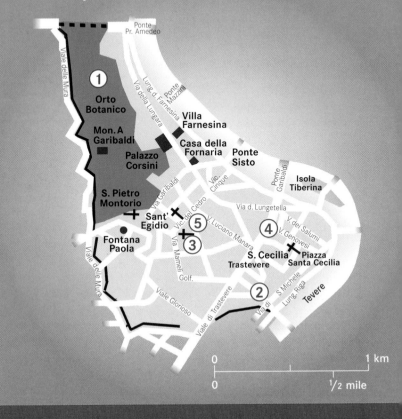

① Gianicolo – Janiculum Hill

Between Trastevere and the Vatican, Rome's highest hill affords the most memorable bird's eye views of the city and is a popular lovers' tryst, especially at sunset. According to one of the oldest legends in Roman mythology, the Janiculum was created by the god Janus (hence its name), who had several children, one of whom – Tiber – gave his name to the river below. **Page 127**

② Pick up a bargain

Sick of all the unaffordable, *haute couture* boutiques in central Rome? Then come bargain-hunting at the vast Sunday morning flea market at Porta Portese, famous throughout all of Italy.You name it, you'll find it here, from antiques, books, second-hand clothes and fake Fendi handbags to lingerie, refrigerators and kittens. **Page 129**

③ Santa Maria in Trastevere

Of the many historic churches in this ancient district, Santa Maria in Trastevere is undoubtedly the greatest treasure. Its shimmering golden mosaics, adorning both the inside and the outside of the church, count among Rome's finest. **Page 130**

④ Take the pulse of the city

More than any other area, Trastevere is the Rome of the Romans. The streets pulsate with everyday life – children kick footballs around church squares, locals sit gossiping in doorways and laundry hangs over the medieval flower-splashed façades of the ochre-coloured houses. Wander through its maze of tiny atmospheric streets, taking in the many sights, smells, colours and sounds.

⑤ Live it up

This is currently the 'in' district for nightlife, thanks to its trendy cafés, its cosy bars and a host of cheap, cheerful, family-run pizzerias and *trattorie*. Expect to queue for the most popular eateries, then enjoy an after-dinner stroll through the swirl of lively streets, ending your evening in the romantically illuminated Piazza Santa Maria in Trastevere, at the very heart of the district. **Pages 130, 132–133**

Tip

There is a shortcut to the top of Gianicolo hill. Take Via di San Cosimato eastwards out of Piazza di Santa Maria in Trastevere, then turn right onto via Manara until you reach a T-junction. Take the narrow flight of steps ahead of you beside a small fountain up the hill past San Pietro in Montorio, and continue up Via Garibaldi past the Fontana Paola until you reach the summit.

Tourist information

The tourist information booth is in Piazza Sonnino (halfway along Via della Lungaretta). *Open daily 0900–1800 (tel: (06) 58333457).*

Casa della Fornarina/ Romolo restaurant

Via Porta Settimiana 8. Tel: (06) 5813873. Closed Mon and Aug.

Here in this small unassuming house, Raphael courted Margherita, his lover and model, better known as *La Fornarina* (the baker's girl) – the subject of some of his greatest paintings. After years of passion, Margherita was eventually rejected by Raphael on his deathbed as he belatedly strove to repent his life of sin, and took refuge in the convent of Sant' Apollonia in Piazza Santa Margherita nearby. Her house is now the popular Da Romolo restaurant (*see page 132*).

Just outside, the Porta Settimiana, a gate in the Aurelian wall, was built by Emperor Septimius Severus and rebuilt by Pope Alexander VI in the 15th century. Until 1633 it marked the city boundary. Beyond lies the Via della Lungara, a grand avenue widened and repaved by Pope Julius II to mirror his splendid Via Giulia on the opposite bank of the Tiber, and containing some of Rome's finest *palazzi*.

Fontana Paola

Via Garibaldi.

This monumental fountain on Gianicolo Hill (*see page 127*) was commissioned by Pope Paul V in 1612 to commemorate the reopening of an ancient aqueduct built by Emperor Trajan to bring water from Lake Bracciano to the nearby mills which ground Rome's flour.

It was built with columns from the original St Peter's and marble pillaged from the Forum. In 1690 Carlo Fontana replaced the original five small basins with one massive one, which for centuries was used by locals for bathing and washing their vegetables. Every year, during Rome's Summer Festival, the water is stopped, the basin boarded up and the triumphal arches of the fountain converted into a magnificent backdrop for plays and chamber concerts.

Gianicolo

Of all the hills of Rome, Gianicolo Hill, or the *Janiculum*, as it was called in ancient times, commands the best views of the city. In Imperial times it was the centre of a large wine industry and still today the ancient Roman *pizzutelli* grape, unique to this region, grows wild on its slopes.

While on Gianicolo Hill, don't miss the church of San Pietro in Montorio (Via Garibaldi, open daily 0900–1200, 1600–1830), a favourite place for weddings due to its impressive views. In the courtyard, commemorating the spot where St Peter was martyred, is Bramante's Tempietto – a tiny, circular temple erected in 1502, considered a gem of Renaissance architecture.

At the top of the hill, a large park called the Passeggiata del Gianicolo is a popular weekend haunt for families with its cool shaded gardens, merry-go-round, Punch and Judy shows and refreshment kiosks fringing the sunny terrace overlooking the city. It is also filled with monuments to the famous freedom-fighter Giuseppe Garibaldi and his makeshift army of men, who defended the Roman Republic against the French troops sent to restore papal rule here in 1849, in one of the fiercest battles of the struggle for Italian unity. His equestrian statue stands in Piazzale Garibaldi, with his fearsome wife also on horseback, charging into battle nearby. The countless busts dotted around the park represent some of the thousand-plus martyrs of the Risorgimento. Near the Garibaldi monument, a commemorative cannon is fired daily at noon. Just to the south, the Porta San Pancrazio gate building houses a small Museo Centrale del Risorgimento (*tel: (06) 6793598, open Tue, Wed, Thur 0900–1200*).

Palazzo Corsini

Via della Lungara 10. Tel: (06) 68802323. Open Tue–Sat 0900–1900 (1400 on Sat, 1300 on Sun). Closed Mon. Admission: ££.

The history of 15th-century Palazzo Corsini is inextricably linked to the history of Rome. Over the centuries, such distinguished guests as Bramante, Michelangelo, Erasmus, Queen Christina of Sweden (who died here in 1689) and Napoleon's mother, Letizia Bonaparte have resided here. In 1736, it was remodelled into a more princely *palazzo* for Cardinal Neri Corsini, whose architect Ferdinando Fuga designed the façade to be viewed from an angle, since the street is too narrow for a clear frontal perspective.

Today Palazzo Corsini is the headquarters of the Accademia dei Lincei, a learned society founded in 1603 which once counted Galileo among its members. It also houses part of the collection of the Galleria Nazionale d'Arte Antica, the remainder being in Palazzo Barberini (*see pages 96–97*) with notable 16th- and 17th-century canvases by Caravaggio, Murillo, Rubens and Van Dyck.

Behind the palace, part of the grounds were converted into a magnificent **Botanical Garden** in 1883 (*Orto Botanico, Largo Cristina di Svezia 24, tel: (06) 6864193, open Mon–Sat 0900–1830, 1730 in winter; closed Sun and Aug. Admission: ££*), with over 7,000 plants, a rare collection of medicinal herbs and a scented garden for the blind.

Ponte Sisto

When crossing the 'Sistine Bridge', take time to admire the splendid views: St Peter's to the north, the Aventine hill to the south and the Gianicolo straight ahead. The bridge was constructed by Sixtus IV in 1474 to link Trastevere with central Rome, replacing an ancient Roman bridge long since destroyed – a project financed by levying a tax on the city's prostitutes.

Porta Portese

Via Portuense/Via Ippolito Nievo. Open 0630–1300.

Trastevere's biggest crowd pull is its renowned Sunday morning *mercato delle pulci*, one of the largest 'flea markets' in Europe, at the battered Porta Portese archway, just across the Tiber near Ponte Sublicio. Arrive early for the best bargains from several kilometres of jam-packed stalls selling flowers, antiques, second-hand and new clothes, pets, household wares, jewellery, CDs, shoes, bags, pottery – even suitcases to take home your haul. But keep your wits about you, otherwise you might find your stolen wallet up for sale!

Santa Cecilia in Trastevere

Via di San Michelle. Open 0730–1230, 1600–1900 (Crypt: Tue, Thur and Sat 1130–1230). Admission: £ (Crypt: ££).

Before entering the church of St Cecilia, pause in the courtyard to admire the rose garden russet Baroque façade and its leaning Romanesque tower. St Cecilia lived in a house on this site before being martyred in AD230. After surviving an attempt to scald her to death in the *caldarium* (hot baths), she was beheaded but even then, managed to live a further three days. In front of the altar is Maderno's brilliant statue of her miraculously un-decomposed remains, as seen when she was briefly disinterred in 1599.

Foreigners find a certain serenity in Rome. ,,

berto Moravia,)th-century man novelist

129

Despite this gruesome story, the interior of the church is a sanctuary of calm with piped hymns to remind us of Cecilia's role as the patroness of music. A fine ninth-century mosaic in the apse shows Pope Paschal (who built the church) offering the building to Christ. Hidden in the labyrinth of vaulted rooms and passageways of the crypt is Cavallini's fresco *The Last Judgement*, a veritable masterpiece of Gothic art.

Santa Maria in Trastevere

Piazza Santa Maria in Trastevere. Open 0700–1300, 1530–1900. Admission: £.

This beautiful basilica is one of the oldest churches in the city, the only church to have retained its medieval appearance and the first to be dedicated to the Virgin. It was founded in AD 222 on the site of a miraculous fountain of oil which, according to legend, sprang from nowhere the day Christ was born.

Its present appearance dates from the 12th century, the work of *Trasteverino* Pope Innocent II, although the arched portico with its papal statues was added 500 years later. In the apse, the gleaming gilt mosaic of the *Virgin and Child Enthroned* shows Innocent donating the church to the Virgin. The choir contains a further six mosaics – bold, innovative works by Cavallini depicting episodes from the *Life of St Mary*.

The delicate 12th-century mosaic on the façade (also by Cavallini) shows Mary feeding baby Jesus flanked by ten maidens with lamps, and two tiny unidentified bearers of gifts (one is possibly the artist) kneeling at the Virgin's feet. Gleaming in the sunshine, this golden mosaic provides a stunning backdrop for **Piazza Santa Maria** in Trastevere, a popular meeting-place both day and night, and an ideal spot to while away the hours beside its refreshing octagonal fountain or in one of the cafés, drinking *espresso*, writing postcards or simply soaking up the atmosphere of Trastevere.

Sant' Egidio in Trastevere (Museo del Folklore)

Piazza San Egidio 1b. Open Tue–Sat 0900–1900, Sun 0900–1300. Closed Mon. Admission: ££.

Few museums bring Rome's past to life as vividly as this small folklore museum in the former convent of San Egidio, with its unique collection of paintings, prints and artefacts. Children especially love the life-sized tableaux with waxwork figures portraying daily life in Trastevere – for centuries a village on the city outskirts (the name means 'across the Tiber), settled by sailors, tradesmen, artists and whores, which still today maintains a character and dialect all of its own. The proud people of Trastevere – the *Trasteverini* – consider themselves direct descendants of these ancient tradesmen and continue to lead a very Roman way of life, retaining their ancestor's traditions and customs amid an increasingly chic, international community.

Villa Farnesina

Via della Lungara. Open 0900–1300. Closed Sun. Admission: ££.

This simple early Renaissance villa was designed as a pleasure palace for the rich papal banker and patron of the arts, Agostino Chigi, on the site of the house where Caesar used to entertain Cleopatra. Here, Chigi would host extravagant banquets for all the most distinguished artists, poets, intellectuals, princes and popes, reputedly tossing the silver plates into the river after every course, only to fish them out again from large nets just under the surface of the water after the guests had left.

In his heyday Chigi crammed the villa with works of art, but later sold many to pay off his debts. In 1577 he went bankrupt and sold the villa to the Farnese family. Thankfully, it still contains its fine frescoes, notably Peruzzi's *trompe l'oeil* portrayal of Rome, Sodoma's *Marriage of Alexander and Roxanne* and Raphael's celebrated masterpieces *Galatea* and *The Three Graces* (in which he used Chigi's mistress as one of his models).

131

Dying for love

Raphael was commissioned to execute considerably more painting in Villa Farnesina, but he was so in love with the beautiful La Fornarina (see page 126) that he was unable to concentrate on his work, eventually 'killing himself by over-exertion as he continued his amorous pleasures to an inordinate degree' (Vasari, biographer).

Restaurants and cafés

Alberto Ciarla
Piazza San Cosimato 40. Tel: (06) 5818668. £££. Closed Sun and lunchtimes. A classic fish restaurant with a refined atmosphere and impeccable service, located in one of Trastevere's most picturesque squares.

Checco er Carettiere
Via Benedetta 10. Tel: (06) 5817018. £££. Closed Sun evening. Dine *al fresco* in the garden at one of Trastevere's oldest inns. Delicious home cooking.

Il Forno Amico
Piazza San Cosimato 53. No tel. Closed Sun. Arrive around 1130 and join the crowds of Trasteverini queuing for a ritual mid-morning snack fresh from the oven – *pizza bianco* – baked dough brushed with oil and sprinkled with salt and rosemary. Delicious!

Ivo a Trastevere
Via di San Francesco Ripa 158. Tel: (06) 5817082. £. Closed Tue and lunchtimes. Don't be put off by appearances. This ordinary-looking pizzeria serves some of the best pizzas in town.

Romolo nel Giardino della Fornarina
Via Porta Settimiana 8. Tel: (06) 5818284. ££–£££. Closed Mon and August. A Roman institution and the home of Raphael's celebrated mistress and model, La Fornarina (*see page 126*). Reserve a table in the tiny garden framed by the ancient walls of Rome.

Sacchetti
Piazza San Cosimato 61. No tel. £. Closed Mon. One of Rome's best cafés. Don't miss the *gianduia* (hazelnut) ice-cream or the sinful *sfogliatello di ricotta* (pastries filled with ricotta cheese).

Treat the children in Trastevere with such delights as the fruit-flavoured grattachecca *(crushed ice topped with syrup) at the* Sora Mirella *kiosk on the riverbank near Ponte Cestio, then head up Janiculum Hill to the open-air puppet theatre (* see page 175 *).*

Shopping

Stuck for present ideas? You will easily solve the problem in Trastevere's many small and unusual boutiques. Start with the artisan's workshops in Via dei Vascellari*,* Via dei Salumi *and* Via Santo Cecilia*, and the shops along Via della Lungaretta which specialise in leather and jewellery. Don't miss* Azi *(* Via di San

Nightlife

Trastevere has long been one of the spots for Roman nightlife, crammed with tiny, intimate bars and lively pulsating nightclubs, especially in the area around Piazza dei Ponziani. Latino music is currently in and can be heard at such popular bars as Mambo (Via dei Fienaroli 30) and Yes Brazil (Via San Francesco a Ripa 103), which promises three hours of live music nightly.

Angelo Azurro
Via Cardinale Merry del Val 13. Tel: (06) 5800472. Open Fri–Sun 2400–0400. This age-old gay disco is back in the limelight again, attracting celebrated DJs from around Italy.

Big Mama
Vicolo San Francesto a Ripa 18. Tel: (06) 5812551. Open Tue–Sat 2100–0130. One of the most popular R and B venues in town.

Bistrot les Artistes
Via Montecchi 6. Tel: (06) 5814308. Open Tue–Sun 2100–0200. This tiny haunt dedicated exclusively to cabaret provides a fun night out, even if you don't speak Italian.

Stardust
Via de'Renzi. By day this cosy little bar serves delicious brunches. In the evenings it is jam-packed with locals, with live music sessions every Tuesday.

Selarum
Via dei Fienaroli 12. One of Trastevere's most popular bars for a late night drink, especially in summer when couples sit long into the night in its charming candlelit garden.

Francesto Ripa 170) with its strikingly original collection of rustic pottery and home accessories or Modi e Materie (Vicolo del Cinque 4) for local crafts from the Lazio region, the Porta Portese flea market (see page 129 *) or the morning market at Piazza San Cosimato with its mouth-watering array of regional taste treats!*

A Rome with a view

It is surprisingly easy to get lost in Rome. First there is the traffic and constant hubbub of urban life to contend with. As Bill Bryson wrote in Neither Here Nor There *(1991):* 'I know Rome is dirty and crowded and the traffic is impossible, but in a strange way that's part of the excitement…Rome is so wondrously chaotic.' *Then there are the mazes of narrow streets and alleyways to lose your way in. And, if that is not enough, just as you start to get orientated, you will discover the myth that Rome was built on seven hills. Actually there are twelve!*

TRASTEVERE

The Seven Hills of Rome

Stand atop the Gianicolo, the highest of Rome's hills (but
not one of the fabled seven!), and on a clear day you will be
able to make out the 'Seven Hills' of *Roma intra muros*
(Rome within the ancient city walls) – in anticlockwise
order: Capitolino (the smallest and most famous, site of
ancient Rome's greatest temple), Palatino (where, according
to legend, Romulus and Remus founded the city), Aventino
(today one of the most elegant areas in Rome, with sweeping
river views), Celio (a parkland oasis in the heart of the city,
south of the Colosseum), Esquilino (topped by Santa Maria
Maggiore, a main pilgrimage centre) and Quirinale (home
of the President of Italy), with tiny Viminale squeezed in
between. Originally, they were all much higher, but centuries
of building and accumulated dirt has raised the ground
level in the valleys. But their peaks count among the best
vantage points for admiring Rome's wonderfully-preserved
skyline and for revealing undiscovered treasures and new
aspects of such familiar landmarks as the Forum, the
Colosseum and St Peter's.

Viewpoints

Rome's other hills include Monte Vaticano, from which the
Vatican takes its name, Pincio (a great place to watch the
sun set over the terracotta rooftops) and Monte Testaccio –
Rome's largest rubbish tip – a 50m mountain composed
entirely of broken fragments of over 50 million earthenware
jars. Other noteworthy panoramas can be found at the top
of Castel Sant' Angelo, from the top-floor restaurant of Hotel
Hassler overlooking the Spanish Steps and from the roof
of St Peter's.

The Vatican

The world's smallest country, but with its own stamps, currency, government, media, railway and police force, the Vatican boasts, in St Peter's

IN HONOREM PRINCIPIS APOST PAVLVS V BVRG

Basilica, St Peter's Square and the Vatican Museums, the world's largest church, piazza and museum. It is hardly surprising that this 'City of Popes' is at the top of most visitors' 'must-see' lists as a destination of both religious and artistic pilgrimage.

S·ROMANVS·PONT·MAX·AN·MDCXII·PONT·VII

THE VATICAN

The Vatican

Getting there: **By metro:** The quickest way to reach the
Vatican district is by Metro A to Ottaviano. This stop is
especially convenient for the Vatican Museums and about
a ten minute walk north of St Peter's. **By bus:** Bus No. 64
goes from Piazza dei Cinquecento (in front of Termini
railway station) to St Peter's, via Piazza Venezia and Corso
Vittorio Emanuele II. Other useful routes include No. 23
from Trastevere, No. 81which passes near the Colosseum,
Piazza Venezia, Piazza Navona, the Pantheon and Piazza
del Popolo, and No. 492 via Piazza Barberini and Il Corso,
all of which stop in Piazza del Risorgimento. A little shuttle
bus ferries tourists between St Peter's and the Vatican
Museums every half-hour, taking a scenic shortcut through
the Vatican gardens.

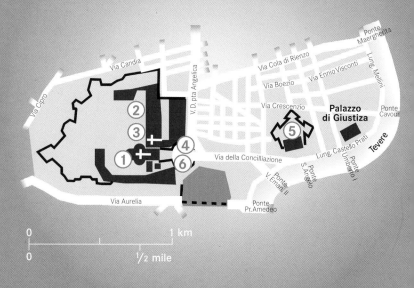

① St Peter's

Visiting the greatest church in Christendom, with its awe-inspiring dimensions and magnificent art treasures, is always a moving experience. The long climb to the top of the dome is rewarded by stunning views of Rome and the Vatican City. **Pages 146–147**

② Vatican Museums

The Vatican Museums make up the world's largest museum complex: 1,400 rooms containing priceless works of art commissioned and collected over the centuries by the wealthy pontiffs. On a first visit, it is best to limit the number of collections you explore, but don't miss the Pio-Clementine Museum, the Raphael Rooms and the Sistine Chapel. **Pages 142–145**

③ The Sistine Chapel

Over twenty thousand people visit the Sistine Chapel daily. To enjoy one of Rome's most visited sights in relative solitude, arrive well before the museum opens and queue. When the doors open, grab the lift on the left in order to beat the crowds racing up the spiral staircase to the ticket office, then run straight to the Chapel, leaving the other collections till later. And remember your binoculars! **Pages 144–145**

④ Meet the Pope

To attend a Papal Audience (usually held on Wednesdays at 1030), apply for tickets in writing a couple of weeks in advance to the *Prefettura della Casa Pontifica, 00120 Citta del Vaticano (tel: (06) 69883017).*

⑤ Castel Sant' Angelo

The layers of two millennia of history are brought to life in this famous wedding-cake castle, built as a mausoleum for Emperor Hadrian, and subsequently used as a fortress, a papal palace, a prison, a place of execution, an air-raid shelter and now a museum. What's more, the views from its parapets are absolutely dazzling. **Pages 140–141**

⑥ Post your postcards here

If you are only staying a short time in Rome, your letters and postcards will invariably arrive home after you, unless you post them here at the Vatican Post Office – reputedly faster than the Italian mail service, although that's not saying much! **Page 151**

Tip

Visiting the Vatican can be a tiring experience, so make it easy for yourself and choose your times carefully. Try to avoid Easter and August, when such confined spaces as the Sistine Chapel can be unbearably crowded. The last Sunday of the month (when entry to the Vatican Museums is free) is always jam-packed, as are Mondays, when the majority of Rome's museums are closed.

139

Tourist information

The Vatican's tourist information office (Ufficio Informazioni Pellegrini e Turisti) is on the south side of Piazza San Pietro. *Open Mon–Sat 0830–1900 (tel: (06) 69884466).*

Castel Sant' Angelo

The cylindrical bulk of this landmark has dominated the Tiber since Hadrian constructed his mausoleum here in AD 130. Over the years, its mighty brick walls, stripped of their marble and pitted by cannonballs, have survived a remarkably chequered history. In the Middle Ages, it was Rome's mightiest military bastion and throughout the Renaissance served as a palatial hideout for popes in troubled times, linked to the papal apartments by a kilometre-long secret passageway – the Vatican Corridor – that snaked through the walls of the Vatican.

Once inside the castle, Hadrian's impressive spiral ramp, still with traces of original black and white paving, leads up to a bridge over the funerary chamber where the ashes of emperors were stored in urns, and into the **Angel's Courtyard** (Cortile dell'Angelo) – once the castle's ammunition store – stacked with tidy piles of cannonballs and guarded by a marble angel (originally on top of the castle). A small chapel (with a façade designed by Michelangelo) and a military museum open off the courtyard, as well as a labyrinth of corridors leading to the papal apartments.

Luxury apartments

Even in times of siege, the popes made sure that they were not without their comforts. Their luxurious apartments contain lavish wall frescoes, ornate chimney-pieces and ceilings by such celebrities as Dossi, Poussin and Lotto. The

height of luxury was enjoyed in the **Papal Bathroom**, where every inch of wall and even the side of the bath is smothered in delicate designs. The water for the marble bathtub was heated by a log fire under a giant caldron hidden behind the wall. The Vatican's most precious possessions – papal jewels and crowns – were once stored in the castle in the **Room of the Secret Archives**, until 1870 when the new Italian government claimed the fortress as state property.

Leading down from the **Courtyard of Alexander VI**, used for theatrical performances in its heyday, are the dreaded dungeons of the Historic Prison, where such famous prisoners as sculptor Benvenuto Cellini and philosopher Giordano Bruno wasted away in cramped, gruesome conditions, before being tortured to death or murdered in their cells. The third floor of the castle boasts still more luxurious rooms and **Paul III's Loggia** which surrounds the entire building, affording tremendous views in every direction.

Tosca

Opera buffs will recognise the **Terrace** atop the entire ensemble as the final scene in Puccini's tragic opera *Tosca*, with its giant 18th-century bronze statue of Michael, the Archangel. The castle gained its name in 590 after Pope Gregory the Great had a vision of the Archangel Michael hovering over Hadrian's tomb and sheathing his sword to signal the end of a terrible plague. In July 1992, a live television production of the opera was shot on location with each scene performed at the time of day specified in the libretto, climaxing at 0500, when millions of viewers in 107 countries watched Tosca hurl herself to her death from these very battlements. The film was a huge success, unlike one early New York performance, when the heroine leapt from the stage-set Castel Sant' Angelo onto an over-taut trampoline, accidentally bouncing back on stage to rapturous applause!

Getting there: Lungotevere Castello. Open 0900–1900. Closed: public holidays and the second and fourth Tue of each month. Admission: ££.

Musei Vaticani I

At first, it seems ironic that the world's smallest country should contain the world's largest museum. But consider the extravagance of the Catholic Church over the centuries and the volumes of priceless art commissioned by its many popes, and the mile upon mile of priceless collections, from ancient Etruscan statuary to Picasso paintings, crammed into 1,400 rooms will perhaps come as less of a surprise.

Where to start? Remember Stendhal's wise words: 'If the foreigner tries to see everything … he will develop a furious headache, and presently satiety and pain will render him incapable of any pleasure'. First-timers are well advised to concentrate simply on the Pio-Clementine Museums, the Raphael Rooms, the Pinacoteca galleries and the Sistine Chapel. In getting to these, you will get a taste for other collections – Greek, Roman and Etruscan sculptures, modern religious art, books, maps, clocks, tapestries, gold jewellery and sumptuous papal apartments frescoed by the greatest artists of the times – as you wend your way through the vast labyrinth of corridors and galleries that were originally papal palaces built for such Renaissance pontiffs as Sixtus IV, Innocent VIII and Julius II.

To help control the flow of visitors the Vatican has devised four colour-coded one-way paths through the collections, varying in length from 90 minutes to 5 hours. All pass through the Sistine Chapel (route A most directly).

Museo Pio-Clementino

This museum boasts a staggering collection of ancient Greek and Roman art and antiquities, salvaged during the

16th century from ancient monuments ruthlessly dismantled to make way for Renaissance Rome. It includes the elegant *Apollo Belvedere* torso which so influenced Michelangelo and, most celebrated of all, the remarkable first-century BC *Laocoön* group, uncovered in 1506 on the Esquiline Hill, depicting the Trojan priest and his two sons fighting off the snakes sent by Athena to kill them.

Pinacoteca Vaticana

The fifteen-roomed Picture Gallery sometimes gets short shrift, situated near the exit and full of weary visitors. This is a shame, as it contains a remarkable collection of canvases spanning ten centuries. Among the most important exhibits are works by Giotto, Fra Angelico, Lippi, Bellini's *Pietà*, Leonardo da Vinci's unfinished *St Jerome* in sombre sepia tones, Raphael's *Coronation of the Virgin* (one of his first works) and *Transfiguration* (his last great work), Veronese's moving *Sant' Elena*, Caravaggio's dramatic *Descent from the Cross* and Melozzo da Forli's ethereal frescoes of *Musician Angels*.

Stanze di Raffaelo

During the Renaissance, parts of the museums were decorated with sumptuous frescoes, including the four Raphael Rooms containing the young artist's greatest works in Rome, commissioned by Pope Julius II.

" *After a day of the papal renaissance and baroque, and of the great ancient walls of brick which being of brick often look as though they are not ruins but being built now by builders gone on strike – all one desires is a bidet of caffè granita [frozen, grated coffee] to bathe the feet in.* "

William Sansom, *Grand Tour Today*, 1968

Getting there: Città del Vaticano (entrance to the north in Viale Vaticano). Tel: (06) 6983333. Open 16 Mar–30 Oct Mon–Fri 0845–1545, Sat 0845–1245. Also, for all other periods of the year, Mon–Sat and the last Sunday of the month 0845–13.45. Closed public and religious holidays and Sundays (except the last Sun of each month). Admission: £££ (free the last Sun of the month). Headset guides available at the museum entrance (££).

Musei Vaticani II

Stanze di Raffaelo (continued)

Raphael's most noteworthy frescoes, in the **Sala della Segnatura** (1509–11), show the epitome of his classical style, full of rich colours and with clever use of light and space, particularly apparent in the *Dispute over the Holy Sacrament* and the acclaimed *School of Athens* fresco opposite, portraying ancient characters with the features of contemporary heroes – bearded Plato in the centre is Leonardo da Vinci, pensive Heraclites on the steps is Michelangelo, and to his right is Bramante, dressed as Euclid. Those in the **Stanza d'Elidoro** (1512–13), show the artist's development from High Renaissance art in *The Miracle of Bolseno* (over the window to the left) to a more powerful and realistic style in *The Liberation of St Peter*, where Pope Julius II is portrayed as the saint himself – some of the finest artworks in the museum.

Capella Sistina

Nothing can prepare you for the visual impact of the recently-restored Sistine Chapel, one of the most visited sights in Rome, attracting over 20,000 visitors daily. On the ceiling of the chapel, Michelangelo (totally new to fresco techniques!) laboured painstakingly for four years (1508–12) to create what is today considered the greatest painting ever produced.

It is an astonishingly elaborate work based on Old Testament scenes from the Creation to the Salvation of Noah, none more famous than the *Creation of Adam* in the centre, with the celebrated outstretched fingers. Michelangelo began his oeuvre near the entrance and ended it over the altar.

Benches are provided for viewing the ceiling from different perspectives. Remember to take binoculars and see whether you can spot the point (somewhere about midway) where experts agree that the great sculptor became more assured with his new painting techniques, and started to produce bolder, more heroic and expressive figures. Around the walls, various biblical scenes have been added by other great masters of the Renaissance including Botticelli, Signorelli, Ghirlandaio and Perugino.

> " *Sauntering around the Vatican, I wilted from exhaustion, and when I got home, my legs felt as if they were made out of cotton.* "
>
> **Anton Chekhov (in a letter to a friend in Moscow after his Vatican visit)**

The brilliant lapis-blue *Last Judgement* fresco on the altar wall was also painted by Michelangelo, 23 years after finishing the ceiling. Demonstrating his belief that suffering is a vital stage in the search for faith in God, it depicts the souls of the dead rising up to face the wrath of Jesus, with the good promoted to heaven, and the damned cast into the abyss of hell. This harrowing subject, rarely used as an altar backdrop, was chosen by the Pope as a warning to Catholics to heed their faith despite the turmoil of the Reformation. Michelangelo's self-portrait can be spotted on the flayed skin held by the martyr St Bartholomew at Christ's feet.

Other attractions

If you have time, try and fit in three other museums: the Egyptian Collection, the Etruscan Collection and the Gregoriano Profano Museum, which includes the Athlete mosaics from the Baths of Caracalla.

And as you go round, make sure you glimpse the Vatican Gardens through the windows, covering over a third of the Vatican's acreage with their woodland, fountains, Vatican Radio studios, railway station and even a cabbage patch, essential fare for today's Polish Pope. *Garden tours require advance reservation through the Tourist Information Office, tel: (06) 69884466.*

Piazza San Pietro

St Peter's Square is surely the most theatrical of all Rome's piazzas, its semicircular **colonnaded wings** representing the outstretched arms of the Church, symbolically embracing the faithful. Built in 1656 on the site of Nero's ancient circus (where many early Christians were martyred) for Pope Alexander VII, by the brilliant Baroque architect, Bernini, it took 11 years to complete the swirl of pillars and the 140 statues of saints and martyrs which encircle the square. The square is adorned by **two Baroque fountains** and a red granite **obelisk** brought from Egypt by Caligula in AD 37, topped by an iron cross containing a relic of the Holy Cross. Stand on one of the two circular paving stones in the middle of the square, and delight in Bernini's contrivance to make the quadruple rows of perfectly-aligned columns appear as one.

The finished result provides a spacious meeting place for countless thousands of pilgrims. On Easter Sunday as

many as 300,000 people cram into the square for the Pope's **traditional open-air service**. He also usually blesses the crowds at Mass on Sunday mornings from the balcony of the Apostolic Palace where he lives and works (above the northern colonnade).

San Pietro in Vaticano

Piazza San Pietro. Open 0700–1800, 1900 in summer. Strict dress code. Admission: £ (££ to climb the dome, open 0800–1600, 1800 in summer). Visits to the necropolis under the basilica and St Peter's tomb can be made by prior arrangement by phoning (06) 69885318.

'At Florence you think; at Venice you love; at Naples you look; at Rome you pray.' Nowhere is this old Italian proverb more appropriate than in St Peter's, the world's most important church and the spiritual capital of Roman Catholicism.

The first St Peter's was built by Constantine around AD 326 on the site where St Peter was buried following his crucifixion in AD 64. In the 16th century, Bramante was commissioned to design a completely new basilica. Its construction took over a 100 years, with most of the great architects of the day playing a part: **Michelangelo** designed the lofty dome with help from Fontana and Porta, **Carlo Maderno** built the façade and **Bernini** constructed twin towers to frame the entrance (later torn down when one tower was found to be causing the basilica to crumble).

The overwhelming size and decorative splendour of the breath-taking interior is hard to comprehend, designed for grand papal processions and pilgrimage-sized congregations. Look closely and you will see the lengths of other basilicas marked along the floor of the nave – all much shorter than St Peter's! Bernini's massive gilded bronze *baldacchino*, or altar canopy (under which only the Pope can celebrate Mass) rises six storeys over the high altar and the crypt. His *Throne of St Peter in Glory* in the apse is masterfully illuminated by a central yellow window, portraying the **Dove of Peace** amid rays of sunlight, clouds and flights of angels. Other **noteworthy treasures** include numerous elaborate papal tombs, a 13th-century bronze statue of St Peter whose foot has been worn away by the touch of pilgrims, and Michelangelo's moving *Pieta*, completed when he was just 25 years old and protected by glass since it was damaged in 1972.

147

Via della Conciliazione

Built to symbolise the reconciliation of the Holy See and the Italian State (as sanctioned by the Lateran Treaty of 1929), this broad thoroughfare has received more criticism than any other in Rome. It was constructed by Benito Mussolini in 1936 as part of a grandiose urban development scheme to make Rome 'appear wonderful to the whole world, immense, orderly and powerful as she was in the days of the first Empire of Augustus'.

In the process, Mussolini obliterated an entire medieval quarter and several churches. It was argued that the end result ruined the impact of Piazza San Pietro, originally entered from a narrow medieval street. However, it had been on the papal agenda for centuries to create a monumental approach road to St Peter's and the austere yet majestic façades of Mussolini's **grand avenue** surprisingly provide the ideal foil to Bernini's elaborate curves.

THE VATICAN

The buildings

Look closely and you will notice that the street is not in perfect line, even though some of its original buildings were deliberately sliced back to create the thoroughfare. This problem was rectified, however, by the addition of two straight rows of street lights set on ugly modern, white obelisks. On the façades of the southernmost buildings, the arms of Pope Pius XII symbolically face those of Rome. Other **noteworthy buildings** include the Pius XII Auditorium at No. 4, a Vatican property leased to Rome's Santa Cecilia symphony orchestra, and the Santa Maria in Traspontina at No. 14, the only church in Rome that, until recently, ran a cinema in its refectory.

Palazzo Torlonia at No. 30 boasts the handsomest façade in the street (a replica of the Cancelleria palace near Piazza Campo de' Fiori), and is owned by Prince Torlonia, reputedly the richest man in Rome. Next door, at No. 34, Raphael died in **Palazzo dei Convertendi**, having been forcibly separated from his lover, La Fornarina (*pages 126 and 131*). The building was dismantled to enable construction of the road, then reassembled here. **Palazzo dei Penitenziere**, opposite at No. 33 (today a hotel and restaurant) was built in imitation of Palazzo Venezia (*page 26*) as an Italian cardinal's private residence. The rest of the street is made up of specialised religious bookshops and tourist shops selling everything from John Paul II keyrings to Vatican snowstorms.

> **"** Italian drivers pay no attention to anything happening on the road ahead of them. They are too busy tooting their horns, gesturing wildly, preventing other vehicles from getting into their lane, making love, smacking the children in the back seat and eating a sandwich the size of a baseball bat, often all at once. **"**
>
> **Bill Bryson, *Neither Here Nor There*, 1991**

The Borgo

Via della Conciliazione is one of the city's busiest streets, crammed with cars and tourist buses heading from central Rome to St Peter's. On arriving at St Peter's Square, you have officially left Italy and are in the **Vatican State**. You don't need a passport to enter. Indeed you probably won't even notice the border (although it is marked by a band of white travertine stone running from the ends of St Peter's Square's sweeping colonnades). The surrounding maze of criss-crossing medieval streets – called the **Borgo** (from the Anglo-Saxon *burgh* or 'town) – was traditionally an area of pilgrims' lodgings, monasteries and churches. Today its atmospheric streets are crowded with cafés, restaurants and hotels catering to the tourist trade.

Restaurants and cafés

For the best selection of eateries in the area, steer clear of the overpriced restaurants on Via della Conciliazione and head to the Borgo just beyond – a grid of medieval streets formerly full of pilgrims' lodgings.

Alle Due Fontanelle

Via Federico Cesi 23. Tel: (06) 3612114. ££. Closed Sun lunch. It's easy to miss the entrance to this basement fish restaurant. Once inside the maze of tiny dining rooms, such delectable dishes as fish soup *alla romana* (minimum four people), baked bass with oyster sauce and Sorrento-style anchovies await you.

Caffè San Pietro

Via della Conciliazione 40. Tel: (06) 6864927. £. Closed Mon. This espresso bar-cum-lunch café has gained in notoriety since Ali Agca had a last cup of coffee here before entering St Peter's Square on the day when he tried to assassinate Pope John Paul II.

Enoteca Costantini

Piazza Cavour 16. ££. Closed Sun. Costantini is considered one of the best wine bars, with an impressive selection of wines from Italy and around the world, and ample, tasty snacks to accompany your tastings.

Hostaria da Benito e Gilberto

Via del Falco 19. Tel: (06) 6867769. ££. Closed Sun. Reservation essential. The secret of this humble restaurant's success is its genuine Roman ambiance and simple cuisine – tempting antipasti, grilled fresh fish and mouth-watering desserts.

Macondo

Via Marianna Dionigi 37. Tel: (06) 3212601. ££. Closed Sun and lunchtimes. Ring the changes from Italian cuisine at this bright, lively Caribbean restaurant. You'll find the beef with plantains and avocado hard to resist and the liqueur-saturated banana cake to follow is an absolute must.

Tables with views

For a meal with a view, it's hard to beat Les Etoiles *(Atlante Star Hotel, Via dei Bastioni 1, tel: (06) 6873233, £££) with its fabulous Vatican vistas, while the rooftop café of* Castel Sant' Angelo *(see pages 140–141) makes an excellent light lunch stop with its magnificent views of the Rome skyline.*

Shopping

Via Cola di Rienzo is the main shopping street in the area, a major thoroughfare linking the Vatican with the Tiber, lined with smart boutiques. For affordable high-street fashions, check out **Mötivi** (*No. 254*), **L'Altra Moda** (*Nos. 54–56*) or more sophisticated **Mara and Co** (*No. 275*). Try **Furla** (*No. 226*) for classy handbags, **Mondaddori** (*No. 81–83*) for books and records, **Habitat** (*No. 197*) or **La Residenza** (*No. 36*) for furnishings. Romans consider **Castroni** (*No. 196*) and **Benedetto Franchi** (*No. 204*) to be top-notch delicatessens while tiny, family-run **Tascioni** (*No. 211*) is *the* place to buy fresh pasta, with tortelleni, tortelloni, tonnarello, tagliolini … and at least another 50 different types to choose from.

For ecclesiastical artefacts, concentrate on Via della Conciliazione. Your best bet for books is **Libreria Paoline** (*No. 18*) or **Ancora** (*No. 63*). For Vatican stamps, coins, figurines, jewellery, rosaries, videos and other religious souvenirs, try **Savelli Religiosi** (*Largo del Colonnato 5, opposite St Peter's Square*). For chalices, reliquaries and lay gifts in silver and glass, head to **LMP** at *Via del Mascherino 16*. If you miss the Vatican Museums, do a whistle-stop tour of the highlights in **Edizioni Musei Vaticani** (*Via di Porta Angelica 41*), a small shop selling quality reproduction paintings, posters, calendars, statues and pottery.

Fast delivery

If you're planning to send postcards home, consider posting them at the Vatican Post Office (Piazza San Pietro, tel: (06) 6982, open: Mon–Sat 0830–1800), as Vatican stamps are collector's items and their mail service is reputed to be considerably faster than the Italian one. That said, in a country where lunch frequently takes all afternoon, you'll probably soon stop worrying whether the overseas post takes rather longer than expected.

Nightlife

Auditorium di Santa Cecilia

Via della Conciliazione 4. Tel: (06) 68801044. The city's top symphony orchestra and choir, in existance since the 16th century, reside here in Rome's main classical music venue. In summer they also perform in the grounds of Villa Giulia (*see pages 177–178*).

Azzuro Scipioni

Via degli Scipioni 82. Tel: (06) 39737161. A *cinema d'essai* or 'art-house cinema' (*see page 177*), and one of the main venues showing films in their original language.

Fonclea

Via Crescenzio 82a. Tel: (06) 6896302. This tiny basement pub has live soul, folk or country music most nights and a happy hour from 1900–2000.

New Mississippi Jazz Club

Borgo Angelico 18a. Tel: (06) 68806348. One of the city's trendier jazz venues, with live gigs at weekends and 'video jazz' on other nights.

The Vatican State

The Vatican has been a papal residence for over 600 years, but it has only been a Sovereign State independent of Italy since the signing of the Lateran Pact with Mussolini in 1929. Yet for a country little larger than a golf course (a mere 40 hectares), and with a population of just 500, it boasts wealth and influence far beyond its size. For centuries it was the unchallenged centre of the Western world, a major religious and diplomatic force throughout Christendom and Rome's second political power house, with its own government, statutes, head of state and even its own police force – the famous Swiss guards.

The Swiss role

The exclusive role of the *Cohors Helvetica* is to protect the Holy See. Pope Julius II, impressed by the calibre of Swiss soldiers, first introduced them in 1506 and had their distinctive red, yellow and navy uniforms (the colours of the Medici popes) designed by **Michelangelo**. To qualify, you have to be between 19 and 30 years old, unmarried and Swiss. They are, without doubt, the most photographed figures of the Vatican.

The Pope

The Pope (from the Greek *pappas*, meaning 'father) is absolute ruler of the Vatican and the Catholic Church – a religious community of over 750 million (18 per cent of the world's population). His **official titles** include Bishop of Rome, Vicar of Christ, Successor of the Prince of the Apostles, Supreme Pontiff of the Universal Church, Patriarch of the West, Sovereign of the State of Vatican City and Servant of the Servants of God.

John Paul II

The election in 1978 of the current Pope **John Paul II** (Polish-born Karol Wojtyla), the first non-Italian pope for many years, marked an astonishing break with tradition. Famous for his world tours – which keep alive the physical presence of the papacy around the globe – his humanity, compassion and accessibility are contrasted with his highly conservative attitude, notably his rigid views on such controversial issues as the admission of women to the priesthood, contraception, abortion and homosexuality – topics which, it is claimed, are forcing some Catholics to turn their backs on the Church.

153

Vatican gardens

Further Afield

Churches and mosaics

*This walk explores some of Rome's finest churches and mosaics in the Lateran district and around the Celian Hill. It starts at **San Giovanni in Laterano**, Rome's first Christian basilica, which rivalled St Peter's in splendour in the Middle Ages when the Lateran Palace was the official papal residence.*

The **interior** of San Giovanni is crammed with religious treasures, including the 13th-century apse mosaic which shows Christ when he appeared miraculously during the consecration of the church. Until 1870 all popes were crowned here. Exit San Giovanni on the right near the organ and make for the octagonal **Baptistry of San Giovanni**, which is around the corner and remarkable for its fifth-century green, azure and gold Byzantine-style mosaics.

Leave Piazza di San Giovanni in Laterano along Via di San Giovanni in Laterano, forking left into **Via di Santo Stefano Rotondo**, to a gem of a church after which the street is named, hidden in an oasis of greenery near the end of the road. One of Rome's earliest Christian churches, it is completely circular and contains gory frescoes of martyrs being boiled in oil, stretched and devoured by dogs.

Further down the road, two churches stand side by side: **San Tommaso in Formis** with a 13th-century façade mosaic of Christ flanked by two freed slaves, and **Santa**

Maria in Domnica with its dazzling apse mosaic of Pope Paschal, wearing the square halo of the living, worshipping at the feet of the Virgin and Child. Note the ancient boat-shaped fountain outside the entrance.

Return towards central Rome along Via Celimontana, then first right into Via Annia, and left again into Via dei Querceti. Here steps descend to the fascinating 12th-century **San Clemente**, where dark stairways lead underground through several layers of history to a fourth-century chapel beneath the church, and to ancient Roman remains beyond. The glittering apse mosaic in the main church depicts *The Triumph of the Cross*, set against swirling acanthus leaves and animals.

Cross Via Labicana and walk up Equiline Hill to the small Colle Oppio park overlooking the Colosseum. Turn left, cross through the park, then zig/zag up a series of narrow lanes to **San Pietro in Vincoli**. Here you can view the chains (*vincoli*) supposedly used to shackle St Peter in prison, on display below the high altar, but the church's main claim to fame is Michelangelo's statue of Moses, one of 40 figures planned for the tomb of Pope Julius II, but abandoned for work on the Sistine Chapel's *Last Judgement*.

Follow Via delle Sette Sale around the side of the church past **San Martino ai Monti**, built on the site of a third-century chapel and famed for its early mosaic portrait of Pope St Sylvester. Turn left onto Via Merulana, then left again down Via San Martino ai Monti and first right until you reach jewel-studded **Santa Prassede**, whose chapels contain the most important Byzantine mosaics in Rome.

From here, it is just a short distance down the hill to the magnificent basilica of **Santa Maria Maggiore**, the largest of 80 churches dedicated to the Virgin Mary, with its gleaming mosaics (*see pages 102–103*) prized among the finest in Rome.

INFORMATION

Time:	3 hours
Start-point:	St Giovanni in Laterano
End-point:	Santa Maria Maggiore
Tips:	Do this walk in the morning (or late afternoon on weekdays) as most churches are closed over the lunch-hour. Bring binoculars to study the mosaics in fine detail.

A walk along the Tiber

The Tiber and its island – Isola Tiberina – are the reasons for Rome being founded here, as this was the only place where the river could be crossed with ease and the spot where, according to legend, Romulus and Remus were washed ashore. In imperial times, when a single wooden bridge straddled the Tiber, barges would carry obelisks from Egypt and marble from Tuscany to the very heart of Rome. Nowadays, 26 bridges link Rome with the Vatican, Janiculum and Trastevere.

The walk starts at the unadorned medieval church of Santa Maria in Cosmedin, famed for its celebrated Bocca della Verità (Mouth of Truth), a fierce stone face once used as an ancient well cover, set into the wall of the portico. Medieval pilgrims believed that the mouth would bite the hand of anyone who lied!

Cross Piazza della Bocca della Verità to the Republican Temples of the Forum Boarium. The rectangular temple was dedicated to Portunus, god of rivers and ports, as it was here on the banks around Isola Tiberina that the port of ancient Rome lay. At Ponte Palatino the mouth of the Cloaca Maxima, the city's great sewer, can still be seen and one arch of a ruined bridge dating from 142 BC, known as the Ponte Rotto (broken bridge).

Continue northwards along the riverbank until you reach Piazza Monte Savello and the massive Theatre of Marcellus (*see page 68*). Cross the river via Ponte Fabricio, the oldest functioning bridge in Rome, onto the boat-shaped Tiber Island (*see pages 68–69*).

Continue over the Ponte Cestio, another bridge built in the first century BC, and carve your way through the characterful shopping streets of Trastevere, along Via della Lungaretta to Piazza Santa Maria in Trastevere, graced with the shimmering mosaic-clad Santa Maria in Trastevere (*see page 130*), one of the oldest churches in Rome.

Retrace your steps a short distance, then turn left up Via del Moro to the Fontana Paola (*see page 126*) and back to the riverbank. Cross the river at Ponte Sisto (*see pages 128–129*) and bear left, not along the riverbank, but rather up Rome's very first Renaissance street, Via Giulia. Almost immediately you will pass under an archway spanning the road, part of an unrealised project by Michelangelo to link nearby Palazzo Farnese (*see page 65*) with Villa Farnesina (*see page 131*) on the other side of the river.

Many of the fine palazzi flanking Via Giulia have distinguishing features. Note the two angry-looking stone falcons of Palazzo Falconieri (beyond Santa Maria dell' Orazione e Morte on the left); further up on the right, the façade of Santa Caterina da Siena has pretty yellow reliefs of Romulus and Remus; at the corner of Via del Gonfalone on the left, you can still see part of the foundations of Julius II's planned law courts, curious blocks of travertine nicknamed the 'Sofas of Via Giulia'.

Just past the church of San Giovanni dei Fiorentini at the end of Via Giulia, turn right, cross Corso Vittorio Emanuele II and head up Via Paola to the end of the walk at Ponte Sant' Angelo. This is Rome's most photographed bridge, thanks to the ten windswept angels that stand on top of it, unkindly nicknamed 'Bernini's breezy maniacs' almost as soon as they were sculpted in 1688.

INFORMATION

Time:	2.5 hours
Start-point:	Santa Maria in Cosmedin (Piazza della Bocca della Verità)
End-point:	Ponte Sant' Angelo

Via Appia Antica

Beyond the walled city of ancient Rome, the Appia Antica (Old Appian Way) has experienced more than its fair share of history. Constructed in 312 BC by Emperor Maxentius (and extended by 520km in 194 BC), it was Rome's main link with its expanding empire in the east. In 71 BC, 6,000 of Spartacus's troops were crucified here during a slaves' revolt. It was the route of the elaborate funeral processions of many emperors, the road along which St Paul was led as a prisoner to Rome in AD 56 and where St Peter, fleeing from persecution, encountered Christ and asked 'Domine, quo vadis?' (Lord, where are you going?). More recently, the Fosse Ardeatine nearby was scene of the merciless shooting of 335 innocent civilians shot by the Nazis during World War II.

Today this remarkable road, lined with cypresses and pines, cuts through fields of wild flowers against the picturesque backdrop of the Alban hills to the south. The landscape has changed little since the ancient Romans came here by torchlight to bury their dead since, by law, no burial could take place within the city walls. On either side of the road lie the scattered remains of family tombs and collective burial places known as *columbaria*.

Beneath the fields lies a vast network of Christian catacombs. Finding space for burials was a serious problem in early Christian times so they created underground, multi-layered cemeteries in the soft tufa stone here, some as deep as six storeys. Six million bodies were buried here. Nowadays these damp, musty honeycombs of tunnels and chambers adorned with early Christian paintings and carvings are largely empty of their tombs; it is time-consuming to visit all of them, so settle for just one, then spend the rest of your time enjoying the surrounding countryside. **San Callisto** is the largest catacomb open to the public (with 23km of galleries), famous as the burial place of Santa Cecilia (*see page 129*) and many early popes, while the bodies of the Apostles Peter and Paul are said to have been hidden for several years at the **Catacombs of San Sebastiano** during early Christian persecutions.

Bus ride and walk

Take bus No. 218 from San Giovanni in Laterano to the Appian Way, which starts at the **Porta San Sebastiano**, the largest and best-preserved gateway in Rome's ancient walls. By the church of **Domine Quo Vadis?**

(where St Peter met Christ), the bus branches right down Via Ardeatina. Get off the bus at the Fosse Ardeatine, near the **Catacombs of Domitilla**. Walk along Via delle Sette Chiese to rejoin the Appian Way at the **Catacombs of San Sebastiano**. On the opposite side of the road, beside the tomb of Romulus (son of Maxentius), is a well-preserved **chariot-racing stadium**. Turn right and continue up hill to the cylindrical **tomb of Cecilia Metella** (wife of Crassus, financier of Julius Caesar's early campaigns), unusual in that it became a fortress in medieval times. From here the traffic lightens considerably, turning Via Appia Antica into a pleasant country lane, still in places with its original, uneven **paving stones** over which the Roman legions marched. Continue along here as far as you wish, past the many pagan tombs, before returning to the tomb of Cecilia Metella to catch bus No. 760 back to the city centre.

INFORMATION

Time:	3 hours (including visit to the catacombs)
Start-point:	Porta San Sebastiano (bus); Fosse Ardeatine (walk)
End-point:	Tomb of Cecilia Metella
Tips:	Bring your own refreshments, and go early, before it gets too hot. On Sundays, the Via Appia is closed to traffic except buses and wedding parties.
Getting there:	Take the No. 218 bus from San Giovanni in Laterano to Porta San Sebastiano. Return on bus No. 760 from the Tomb of Cecilia Metella to Circo Massimo. Better still, hire a scooter!

Villa Borghese I

Villa Borghese Gardens

Porta Pinciana/Via Flaminia. Open daily dawn–dusk. Admission: £.

Rome's largest central park was laid out between 1613 and 1616 at the top end of Via Veneto just outside the Aurelian walls, as the grounds of the Borghese family's summer retreat. Redesigned in the 18th century, following the fashion for 'English parkland', it was the inspiration for Ottorino Respighi's symphonic poem *The Pines of Rome* (1924), and still today its woods and shaded walkways offer a cool retreat from the noisy city.

The park is at its liveliest on Sunday mornings when Roman families stroll in the park, children gather in the playgrounds and the zoo, couples go boating and sun worship in fountain-splashed squares, or watch the colourful pony traps in Piazza di Siena. With an aviary, racetrack (the Galoppatoio) and one of Rome's finest art museums, there is enough to keep the whole family amused for hours.

Galleria e Museo Borghese

Villa Borghese, Piazzale Scipione Borghese 5. Tel: (06)8417645. Open June–Sept, Tue–Sun 0900–1900; Oct–May, Tue–Sat 0900–1700, Sun and holidays 0900–1300. Closed Mon. Admission: £££.

This handsome Baroque villa was designed as a summer retreat for Cardinal Scipione Borghese, to house his small but outstanding **art collection**. He was one of the greatest patrons and collectors of his day, taking full advantage of being the nephew of a pope by ruthlessly persuading owners to part with their most prized masterpieces, and even going to the lengths of stealing paintings that he really coveted. He had Raphael's *Deposition* removed from the Baglioni family chapel in Perugia under cover of night.

His original collection was later plundered by Napoleon, who persuaded Camillo Borghese (his brother-in-law) to hand over the most cherished pieces to the Louvre in Paris. The remainder was acquired by the state in 1902 and is generally considered, after the Vatican Museums, to be Rome's finest collection of Classical and Baroque art.

Closed for renovation for many years, the villa has finally reopened, with sculptures in the splendidly frescoed rooms of the **lower floor** (*the museo*), and all the major paintings hung on the **upper floor** (*the galleria*). Downstairs, there are some important Classical **sculptures** including a *Dancing Faun* and a *Sleeping Hermaphrodite*. Scipione, however, was an enthusiastic patron of Bernini, and it is his works which dominate the museo. Look out for his earliest sculpture, *Aeneas Carried from Troy*, carved when he was a precocious 20 years of age; a determined David, said to be a self-portrait sculpted while Scipione held a mirror, the unfinished *Truth Unveiled by Time*, the *Rape of Proserpine* (notable for the way Pluto's fingers sink into the marble-defying flesh of Proserpine) and his undisputed masterpiece, *Apollo and Daphne*, the graceful water-nymph fleeing the sun god and magically transforming into a laurel tree.

Surprisingly, the museum's sculptural *pièce de resistance* is not a work of Bernini's, but rather Antonio Canova's *Paolina Borghese* – Napoleon's sister and Camillo Borghese's wife – depicted bare-breasted as a naked reclining **Venus**, with her right hand cleverly concealing her ear (her one imperfection!), in a flirtatious pose befitting her scandalous reputation. Amongst society, Paolina excited much gossip, renowned for her flamboyant clothes and jewellery, her lovers and her servants, whom she used as footstools.

The **first floor** contains paintings by celebrated Italian masters of the 16th and 17th centuries, including fine works by Guercino, del Sarto, Veronese, Botticelli, an entire room of Caravaggios (including *Boy with a Fruit Basket*), Raphael's *The Deposition of Christ*, Bassano's *The Last Supper* and Correggio's erotic *Danae*.

163

Villa Borghese II

Galleria Nazionale d'Arte Moderna e Contemporanea

Viale delle Belle Arti, 131. Tel: (06) 322981. Open Tue–Sat 0900–2200, Sun 0900–2000, Closed Mon. Admission: ££.

Fed up with countless museums of ancient Roman remains or Baroque art? Then this gallery, containing Rome's main collection of **modern art** (from 1800 onwards) will make a refreshing change. Just beyond the northwest boundary of Villa Borghese, Cesare Bazzini's dazzling white *Belle Epoque* palace is one of the few remaining buildings erected for the Rome International Exhibition of 1911. The most interesting of the Italian canvases are by the *macchiaioli* (Italy's answer to French Impressionists) and Futurist artists Umberto Boccioni and Giorgio de Chirico, but there are also works by Klimt, Kandinsky, Cezanne, Degas, Van Gogh, Monet, Pollock and Henry Moore. Major temporary exhibitions are also staged periodically.

Villa Giulia – Museo Nazionale Etrusco

Piazza di Villa Giulia 9. Tel: (06) 3201951. Open Tue–Sun 0900–1900.
Closed Mon. Admission: ££.

Near the Galleria Nazionale d'Arte Moderna, on the outskirts of Villa Borghese, is the pretty 16th-century Villa Giulia, housing a world-famous collection of Etruscan and other pre-Roman remains.

The villa was built as a country residence and pleasure palace for Pope Julius III and, together with fine gardens, shady courtyard, pavilions and fountains, designed by the top architects of the time: Michelangelo, Vasari and Vignola. Its façade, loggia and *nymphaeum* (literally 'area dedicated to the nymphs' – a **sunken courtyard** decorated with Classical mosaics, statues and fountains) were frequently copied in later villas throughout Italy and today it makes a delightful setting for this fine museum of Etruscan art. In the garden, there is a reconstruction of an Etruscan Temple, built in 1891.

The Etruscans arrived in Italy at the end of the eighth century BC, settling between the Arno and the Tiber in an area known as Etruria (today's regions of Umbria, Lazio and southern Tuscany). Although much about this pre-Roman civilisation remains a mystery, they helpfully left a wealth of information about their customs and everyday life by burying the personal possessions of the dead with them in their tombs – round stone burial mounds, built like small huts. The villa is crammed with objects unearthed from most of the major excavations in the region, bearing witness to the sophistication of this early civilisation: weapons, decorative vases, religious artefacts, bronze statuettes of warriors in full battle dress, jewellery, mirrors, combs and cooking utensils. Among the museum's most **prized possessions** are two giant terracotta statues of Apollo and Hercules from a temple near Veio, a bronze toilet box decorated with figurines of the Argonauts, a life-size terracotta sarcophagus of a husband and wife reclining on a banqueting couch and a stunning collection of wax and beaded-gold jewellery from Castellani, showing just how little design has changed over the centuries.

Lifestyles

Shopping, eating, children and nightlife in Rome

167

Shopping

Rome is a shopper's paradise. As fashion designer Franca Fendi once remarked: 'Shopping in Rome is a must, a real must for the rich choice of quality products which are such a good example of "made in Italy". There are really very few who leave without a souvenir – an outfit, a purse, a wallet, a bag or even a suitcase into which to throw whatever they picked up during the trip.'

Shopping in Rome means strolling along some of the most beautiful streets of the city, jostling your way round jam-packed **markets**, marvelling at the number of zeros on the price tags of designer outfits, joining immaculately-preened Romans on their evening ritual stroll (*passeggio*), window-shopping and spending lots of money! As a general rule, go for quality rather than bargains, as the **best buys** are invariably at the luxury end of the market. However, hunt hard and you will find such treasures as handmade marbled notepaper, a trendy pasta pot, herbalists' concoctions, beautiful books on art and architecture, Etruscan-style costume jewellery, regional wines, cheeses and olive oil.

Where to shop

If you are planning on doing lots of shopping during your stay, head straight to the city centre, especially the grid of streets around Via Condotti where nearly all of Italy's big name designers have outlets. By contrast, the *centro storico* is peppered with tiny corner-shop-style stores selling art, antiques, mouth-watering fresh fruit and pasta and countless other goodies. Other popular, more affordable shopping streets include the Via del Corso, Via del Tritone, Via Nazionale and Via Cola di Rienzo. The Campo de' Fiori district is still home to craftsmen, artists and furniture restorers, while Trastevere has a clutter of rather more trendy galleries and boutiques.

Roman shops tend to be rather old-fashioned, as the locals prefer to shop in small, **family-run boutiques**, which can guarantee not only top-quality craftsmanship but also a forum for chat. Therefore, don't expect to find many supermarkets and department stores in Rome (although there are several low-price chain stores such as Standa or Upim).

Markets

Bargain-hunters will be unable to resist Rome's colourful flea markets, especially the famous one at Porta Portese (*see page 129*) every Sunday morning, and the weekday market at Via Sannio (near San Giovanni in Laterano) which specialises in new and used clothing. There is a small market for prints, second-hand and antiquarian books at Piazza Fontanella Borghese (daily except Sunday). On Tuesday mornings, you can visit the wholesale plant and flower market, Mercato dei Fiori, at Via Trionfale (*open 1000–1200*). Rome's most atmospheric food market is the lively morning market in Piazza Campo de' Fiori (*see pages 62–63*) – one of the best places in

all of Rome to watch the routine of Roman life and to try some of the region's food specialities. Remember always to barter for your wares!

Antiques

If you are looking for genuine, authenticated antiques, avoid the markets and try the reputable dealers in Via dei Coronari, Via Giulia and Via Babuino, who will provide a certificate of guarantee (*certificato di garanzia*) and will arrange international shipping and other

formalities. Otherwise, explore Via dei Pellegrino and Via dei Cappellari, where bric-à-brac and the occasional original piece can be found amidst the *ateliers* of cabinet-makers, restorers and other craftsmen.

Fashion

Although Milan is the centre of Italian fashion and design, Romans are known throughout the world for their impeccable grooming and carefully tailored appearance. As a result, the city is an important centre for the fashion-conscious with its abundance of *haute couture* boutiques – a veritable alphabet of designers **from Armani to Zegna**. The city also excels in leather goods – bags, gloves, jackets, belts and luggage of the finest quality and design – at glamorous stores such as Gucci and Fendi, where the shopping experience is nearly as pleasurable as the purchases.

Jewellery

Jewellery is a key part of any Roman wardrobe and the city is teeming with jewellery shops. These range from the small artisan studios in the Jewish Ghetto, around Via Giulia and Campo de' Fiori, through the more sophisticated gold- and silversmiths of Via dei Coronari, Via dell' Orso

169

and Via del Pellegrino to Rome's ultimate jeweller, Bulgari on Via Condotti, for the purchase of a lifetime. For the more thrifty, check out the weird and wonderful costume jewellery in some of the trendy fashion boutiques in Trastevere or Via del Governo Vecchio.

Food and wine

Shopping for food is mainly done in the small neighbourhood delicatessens known as *alimentari*. Here you will find delicious food gifts to take home (both *parmesan* and *prosciutto crudo* travel and keep

well), Rome's finest local vintages, the most superior olive oils and the freshest of pastas. They are also brilliant for buying **picnic provisions**. Many also sell bread and will make you up a sandwich from the various cold cuts on display. Try *bresaola* (air-dried beef), *salami piccante* (spicy salami), such local cheeses as *pecorino*, *taleggio* and *provola* and, if you're feeling flush, buy some pickled wild mushrooms or a tiny jar of truffles.

Souvenirs

There is no shortage of mass-produced souvenir kitsch in Rome, especially around Termini station and the Vatican – Trevi Fountain water squirters, Pope John Paul II keyrings and Colosseum ashtrays to name but a few. For tasteful, quality souvenirs try **museum gift shops**, in particular those in the Vatican Museums and Palazzo Barberini. Religious souvenirs can be found in Via di Porta Angelica and Via della Conciliazione near the Vatican, or in Via dei Cestari near the Pantheon, where several shops specialise in silver chalices and religious vestments.

Sale bargains

Sales (*saldi*) don't always offer such bargains as in other major cities. However, the best time to find fashion at an affordable price is during the **summer and winter sales** (mid-July to mid-September and January to mid-March) when many top designers drastically reduce their prices. Others tempt you into their boutiques with such promises as *sconti* (discounts) and *vendite promozionali* (special promotions), but these offers rarely save you any money. Remember, too, that in general, it is not possible to return merchandise for refund or exchange so think carefully before you get carried away by the glamour of Roman shopping and splash out millions of lire on that dream outfit.

Eating out

La Cucina Romana

Of all Italy's great regional styles, *la cucina romana* has one of the strongest personalities. It combines popular Italian culinary traditions

with the hearty country cooking and bold, sun-drenched flavours of the surrounding Lazio and Abruzzi regions, leaning heavily on olive oil, tomatoes, garlic, wild herbs and *pecorino* (a sharp-flavoured cheese made from ewe's milk) – all of which add a distinct texture, taste and fragrance to even the simplest of dishes.

The people of Rome are justifiably proud of their **culinary tradition**. Indeed, eating is one of their main preoccupations and, for any visitor, a summer dinner enjoyed *al fresco* in a tiny, fountain-filled piazza must be one of the city's most pleasurable experiences.

What's in a name?

Rome offers a huge and colourful selection of eateries. Theoretically, the titles *ristorante*, *trattoria* and *hosteria* correspond to descending levels of price, quality and service but, in reality, they relate more to atmosphere. Don't be fooled by appearances: a cramped and starkly-furnished *hosteria* with paper tablecloths and strip lighting may well serve much better (and cheaper!) food than the fancier *ristorante* next door with its romantic lighting and white-frocked waiters. It will also, invariably, offer a jollier, more authentically 'Roman' dining experience. **Beware** the fixed price *menu turistico* offered in so many restaurants, which may seem temptingly cheap – it is usually rather poor quality. Finally, choose your venue carefully – away from the obvious tourist areas. Choice spots are Trastevere and parts of the *centro storico* away from such tourist honey-pots as Piazza Navona and the Pantheon.

The Romans love **pizza** – a quick slice from a fast-food outlet at lunchtime, as a cheap and cheerful dinner, wafer-thin and straight from the *forno a legna* (wood-fired oven) of a *pizzeria*, or as a popular midnight snack after the theatre. For a light bite, try one of the many **stand-up bars** serving sandwiches, slices of pizza and other *tavola calda* (literally 'hot table), a *Vinaio* (wine bar) with quiches, *bruschetta* (tasty toasted bread with savoury toppings), cheese platters and cold cuts, or a *Pasticceria* (cake shop), where drinks are often served at a small bar to accompany the delectable cakes and pastries.

Rome on a plate

Many restaurants spread out their *antipasto* dishes in mouth-watering displays near the entrance, tempting

you inside for sweet *peperone* (marinated peppers), Parma ham with fresh figs, *mozzarella alla caprese* (soft white buffalo cheese with tomato, basil and olive oil), *prosciutto crudo* (cured ham) and *bresaola* (cured beef), *fiori di zucchi* (courgette flowers in batter), *melanzane* (aubergines), *carciofi* (artichokes) and *finocchio* (fennel), all served cold with in a variety of dressings. Spoilt for choice? Order *antipasto misto* and try a little bit of everything!

As in the rest of Italy, **pasta** is a vital part of any Roman menu, and some of the most classic pasta dishes originated here – *spaghetti alla carbonara* (with bacon, eggs, cheese and cream), *penne all'arrabiata* (literally 'angry quills', with tomato and chillis) and *bucatini all'amatriciana* (hollow spaghetti with tomato, bacon, chilli and *pecorino* cheese). Look out too for more unusual types of pasta – *farfalle* (butterflies), *fusilli* (spirals), *conchigliette* (shells), *cappelletti* (small hats) or *gnocchi* (pasta dumplings, traditionally eaten on Thursdays) – there are nearly as many types as days in the year!

Typical **sauces** include *aglio e olio* (garlic, olive oil and chilli pepper), *pesto* (basil, garlic, olive oil, pine nuts and pecorino), *bianco* (just melted butter), *vongole* (clams and tomatoes) and good old *bolognese*. Rice fans should try *risotto alla Romana*, made with liver, sweetbreads, *pecorino* and *Marsala*.

Many genuinely **Roman meat dishes** are based on or around offal, a tradition dating back to ancient times when the patricians ate the meat and the poor got the leftovers. Specialities include *trippa alla romana* (tripe in a rich tomato sauce), *coda alla Vaccinara* (braised oxtail with tomatoes), *ossobuco alla romana* (veal shinbone with tomatoes, onions and mushrooms). Veal is also popular, with Rome's great *saltimbocca* (literally 'jump in the mouth', veal wrapped in raw ham and sage in a Marsala sauce) in pride of place. For something more conventional, try *capretto* (roast kid), *porchetta* (suckling pig) and *abbacchio* (spring lamb), flavoured with sage, garlic and rosemary and served with anchovy paste or, for that special occasion, a feed-a-family-sized *bistecca alla fiorentina* (Florentine steak).

Fish tends to be pricey. Traditional dishes include *sepiette con i carciofi* (cuttlefish with artichokes), *anguillette in umido* (stewed baby eels) and *filetti di baccalà* (cod fillets fried in batter), a popular Roman snack or first course. Look out also for *pesce spada* (swordfish), *spigola* (sea bass) and *fritto misto di pesce* (mixed fried fish).

Roman cuisine boasts a surprising array of seasonal and imaginative **vegetable dishes** – *fave al Guanciale* (broad beans with bacon and onion) in spring, *misticanza* (a fresh mix of salad leaves including peppery *rughetta* or rocket) in summer, *funghi porchini* (plump boletus mushrooms) in autumn and the lime-green, spiralling *broccoli romaneschi* (one of countless varieties of broccoli) in winter.

Those with a **sweet tooth** may be disappointed in Rome. Apart from the ubiquitous *tiramisù*, *crostata di ricotta* (Roman cheesecake) and *zuppa Romana* (the Italian version of trifle), most restaurants simply serve *macedonia* (fruit salad) or a slice of *torte*. Many Romans omit the dessert course and buy an ice-cream from a local *gelateria* instead as part of a late-evening stroll.

Local tipples

Rome's local wine comes from the surrounding province of Lazio, where the rich volcanic soil gives it a special aroma. The most popular whites (both sweet and dry) are the delicious, amber-coloured Castelli Romani wines from the hills southeast of Rome, including the famous region of Frascati. Many *trattorie* serve these Castelli Romani wines **straight from the barrel**

into carafes. House reds come from slightly further afield, and usually include Montepulciano from Abruzzo and Chianti from Tuscany and Umbria. Look out also for the unusually named Est! Est! Est! from Montefiascone, the rich, velvety Barolo and Gattinara wines, and Falerno – already popular in Caesar's time and still a favourite today. **Beer** is increasing in popularity, with Italian beer not as strong as many northern European brands.

Popular after-dinner *digestivi* include Italian **brandy** (*Vecchia Romagna* or *Stock* are the best) or *grappa* – clear, fiery *eau-de-vie* distilled from grapes and flavoured with fruit and herbs. Liqueurs are also popular. Try the sweet, almond-flavoured *amaretto*, *strega* (made from saffron), *amaro* (a bitter medicinal concoction of mysterious herbs) or, for something really unusual, an aniseed-flavoured *sambuca* with a *mosca* (fly) swimming in it – a coffee bean, floating on the surface for added flavour!

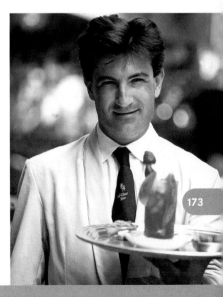

173

Rome with children

Considering that Italians absolutely adore children and spend a lot of time cooing into prams and patting toddlers on the head, Rome offers surprisingly few facilities or entertainment specifically for kids; you will need to use your imagination to the full to keep them amused. Add treats and surprises to the day's itinerary – toss a coin in the Trevi Fountain to make a wish, find the single marble foot (see page 83) in a street near the Pantheon, feed the pigeons or have a caricature painted in Piazza Navona... and if all else fails, kids can always be placated, bribed or simply spoilt with a slab of pizza in a café or an ice-cream from one of the many gelaterie *dotted about town.*

Museums

Most of Rome's museums are decidedly 'hands-off'. However, older children enjoy parts of the **Vatican Museums** (*see pages 142–145*), especially the mummies in the Egyptian Museum, the ancient carved marble animals of the Museo Pio-Clementino (in the Sala degli Animale) and the galleries of huge painted maps and globes en route to the Sistine Chapel. The modest **Wax Museum (Museo delle Cere)** near Piazza Venezia is not exactly Madame Tussaud's, but it is quite fun for a rainy day, as is Trastevere's **Museo del Folklore** with its wax models of Roman life in bygone days. Near the Via Appia Antica, combine a visit to the

Museum of the Walls (Museo delle Mura), housed within the medieval towers of Porta San Sebastiano, with a walk along part of the ancient walls, to provide a new perspective of the city.

Ruins

Of all Rome's ruins, it is always the Colosseum which really captures children's imagination, especially if accompanied with tales of gladiators and wild animals. Outside the arena, a photo taken beside a centurion dressed in leather tunic, thonged sandals, metal breastplates and ancient Roman headgear makes a precious souvenir to show to friends back home. Before visiting the Forum, capture their imagination by purchasing a children's guide to Ancient Rome from a nearby stand. If all else fails, the ancient ruins make a great place to play hide and seek! At Castel Sant' Angelo the prison chambers, trap doors, ramparts, drawbridges and cannonballs are guaranteed to keep kids amused for an hour or two.

Churches

Churches need not be 'boring' if you visit San Clemente and explore the secret corridors and dark stairways beneath the church right down to the city sewers, or take them to Santa Maria in Cosmedin to place their hands into the 'mouth of truth'. The Catacombs and the macabre 'bone church' of Santa Maria della Concezione add a satisfyingly gruesome touch for older children, while everyone enjoys the views from the roof of St Peter's.

Parks

Villa Borghese is one of Rome's most entertaining places for youngsters with its bike hire, pony rides, pedal boats, merry-go-round, children's cinema and zoo. Children simply love the open-air puppet shows on top of Gianicolo hill (every weekday evening in summer and all year round on Sunday mornings). For the best playgrounds, head for Villa Celimontana, Villa Sciarra or Villa Pamphili. And why not ring the changes from travelling everywhere by bus or metro? Take a boat trip on the Tiber (ask at the Tourist Office for information), a horse-and-carriage ride from Piazza di Spagna or a tram ride round the town from Villa Borghese (*see pages 162–163*).

After dark

Rome is a beautiful city by night. Its fountains and façades are softly illuminated, its squares lit with fairy-lights, its streets alive with the chatter of locals on café terraces. Most of the bars, cafés, wine bars and restaurants are located around Piazza Navona and Piazza della Rotonda in the centro storico, *while the best-known discos and nightclubs are concentrated around Trastevere, Via Veneto and most recently the trendy district of Testaccio, with such popular venues as Spago piano bar and Alibi, the funkiest gay club in town.*

Most Romans start their evening out with a drink in a bar or café before a leisurely dinner, followed by an ice-cream as part of a late-evening stroll. They will then proceed to a wine bar *(enoteca)*, piano bar (found in most top hotels, frequently with stunning rooftop views) or a live music venue. Pubs have recently become popular and you will find thriving English- or Irish-style watering-holes dotted about the city.

Discos and clubs

Never arrive before midnight unless you want to have the place to yourself, and remember either to ooze wealth or dress in tomorrow's fashions to get past the choosy bouncers! The choice of late-night spots is not as immense as in some capital cities, but there are nevertheless dozens of dancing venues to suit all tastes and ages. Clubs attract a sophisticated crowd while discos are predominantly for a younger set. Some of the current *in* places include the glamorous **Gilda** nightclub (*Via Mario de' Fiori 97*) and the tiny disco **Notorius** (*Via San Nicola da Tolentino 22*) where, if you can get in, you may find yourself rubbing shoulders with international celebrities. Some clubs require you to take out temporary membership (*tessera*) but, to compensate, the entry price often includes a free drink. During summer months, many discos and clubs close as Roman nightlife moves to the beach resorts south of the city.

For live music, the best jazz clubs are **Big Mama's** (*Vicolo San Francesco a Ripa 18*) and the **New Mississippi Jazz Club** (*Borgo Angelico 18a near the Vatican*). For folk and blues head to **Folkstudio** (*Via Frangipane 42*) or **Akab** (*Via di Monte Testaccio 96*). For rock and pop, Rome is a major destination for the European concert circuit, attracting the biggest stars in the music business to such venues as Stadio Olimpico, Stadio Flamino football stadium and the Palazzo dello Sport in EUR, just south of Rome.

Cinema

Rome – one of the most filmed cities of the world – has a long cinematic tradition, with Cinecittà, Mussolini's 'Cinema City', once producing movies unrivalled outside Hollywood. Naturally, there are numerous cinemas in the city, but they mostly show the latest releases dubbed into Italian (when a film is not dubbed it will be advertised as

versione originale or *VO*). The tiny **Pasquino** cinema in *Trastevere* (*Vicolo del Piede 19*) is Rome's only all-English cinema, otherwise look out for art-house cinemas (*cinema d'essai*) such as **Augustus** (*Corso Vittorio Emanuele 302*) and **Nuovo Sacher** (*Largo Ascianghi 1*), which occasionally show films in their original language.

Classical music and theatre

Attending a classical concert is one of the most pleasurable ways to spend an evening in Rome, thanks to the abundance of concerts and variety of settings – churches, concert halls, palaces, villas and, in summer, open-air venues such as parks, piazzas, gardens and ancient ruins. The main concert season runs from October to June, with special summer programmes for the rest of the year. Look out for concerts in Piazza del Campidoglio or the grounds of Villa Giulia during the

177

summer, choral masses in St Peter's throughout the year, and church recitals which are often free. Otherwise, the main concert venues are the **Accademia di Santa Cecilia** (*Via della Conciliazione 4*) and the **Teatro dell'Opera** (*see below*).

Theatre, on the other hand, is less enjoyable unless you speak fluent Italian or the venue itself provides the drama – for instance an open-air venue at an ancient site. Most productions are in Italian and the main season runs from October until early June. Mainstream theatre can be seen at **Teatro Argentina**, Rome's best-known theatre (*Largo Argentina 56*), and musicals at **Teatro Eliseo** (*Via Nazionale 183*) while more avant-garde plays by lesser-known writers and other fringe productions (known as *teatro off*) are staged at Rome University's **Teatro Ateneo** (*Viale delle Scienze 3*) and **Teatro Colosseo** (*Via Capo d'Africa 5a*).

Ballet and opera

The opera season runs from October to June at the **Teatro dell' Opera** (*Via Firenze 62*) and there is also an outdoor summer series at a variety of venues. *Contact the box office free phone line on 167016665 for details*. The theatre also has a resident ballet company, the Corpo di Ballo del Teatro dell'Opera. For modern dance, check out **Teatro Vascelio** (*Via Giacinto Carini 72*).

Listings and tickets

There are several listings magazines to help you find out what's on when. The best include the weekly *Roma C'è* guide (issued every Thursday and containing comprehensive listings for theatre, film, music, dance and nightlife, with a section in English and a 'Children's Corner'), *Time Out Roma* (a monthly listings magazine, written in Italian, but easy enough to understand without any knowledge of the language), *Trovaroma* (a tiny but invaluable cultural supplement that comes with Thursday's edition of *La Repubblica* newspaper) and *Where Rome* (an informative English magazine with advice on shopping, dining and entertainment, which can usually be picked up for free at your hotel reception).

Booking tickets for shows in advance can be difficult, as many theatres do not sell seats to telephone callers. Your best bet is to contact a ticket agency, which will charge a fee to make a booking for you (usually around 10 per cent of the ticket price). Try **Box Office** (*Via Giulio Cesare 88, tel: (06) 3720215*) for classical music, jazz, pop and rock events and **Music Box** (*Via I Persico 78, tel: (06) 5135389*) for theatre, opera, ballet and classical concerts. Opera tickets can also be bought from the box office of the Teatro dell' Opera.

Practical information

PRACTICAL INFORMATION

Practical information

Airports

Rome has two airports: Leonardo da Vinci (also called Fiumicino) handles most of the scheduled flights while the smaller Ciampino airport caters mostly for charter flights. There are direct flights from most major cities in Europe, North America and Australia with Alitalia as the national carrier (*tel: (06) 65631 for information*). In addition, European low-cost airlines such as British Airways' subsidiary company GO are currently offering bargain-rate charter flights. *For further information call Fiumicino on (06) 65951, Ciampino on (06) 794941, Alitalia on (06) 65643 and GO (in the UK) on (0845) 60543231.*

Getting to/from the airport:
Non-stop shuttle trains link Fiumicino with Rome's central railway station, Stazione Termini, 27km away. Trains depart hourly from 0738 to 1008 and the journey takes 30 minutes, arriving at (and leaving from) track 22 at Termini. From here it is a short taxi ride to most hotels. Tickets can be purchased at the ticket window by the platform at Fiumicino, at vending machines at both Termini and Fiumicino and at the Alitalia office near track 22 at Termini (*open 0630–2100*). For night-time arrivals and departures, a night bus runs between Fiumicino and Tiburtina station in the city centre (*for further information call (06) 4775*).

Taking a taxi directly from the airport is considerably more expensive and, traffic permitting, also takes around 30–45 minutes. Make sure you take only licensed (yellow) cabs and agree a price before you start.

From Ciampino, the best way to reach the centre, 13km away, is by taxi. Alternatively you have to catch a COTRAL bus (leaving every half hour) to Anagnina and then take Metro line A to Stazione Termini, but allow an hour and a half for the journey. *For further information call COTRAL on (06) 5915551.*

Airline offices:
Alitalia *Via Bissolati 13 (06) 65643.*
British Airways *Via Bissolati 54 (06) 147858858.*
GO (from the UK) *(0845) 60543231.*
Air New Zealand *Via Bissolati 54, (06) 4880761.*
Qantas *Via Bissolati 35, (06) 486451.*
Delta Airlines *Via Bissolati 54 (06) 4741774.*
TWA *Via Barberini 67 (06) 47211.*
Canadian Airlines *Via Barberini 3 (06) 6557117.*
Aer Lingus *Via Barberini 3 (06) 4818518.*

Climate

Rome has a mild Mediterranean climate, and its southerly position in Europe guarantees over 180 days of sunshine each year. The coldest months (and invariably the quietest) are January and February, with an average temperature of 10°C. Spring and autumn are the best times to visit, as the weather is usually warm and sunny. Even in the evenings it is often mild enough to dine outside. June is the sunniest month, but

CASSA AUTOMATICA/AUTOMATIC PAYMENT STATION

July and August can be unbearably hot and muggy, with sudden thunderstorms and temperatures reaching 40°C. As a result, many Romans leave the city in August, closing down their businesses, shops and restaurants for the month. October is one of the best months for keen photographers, with a high percentage of crisp days and clear skies. The wettest months are November and December.

Currency

Italian currency is the *lira*, abbreviated to '*L*'. Notes come in denominations of L1000, L2000, L5000, L10,000, L50,000 and L100,000. There are L5, L10, L50, L100, L200 and L500 coins, and L200 telephone tokens *(gettoni)* can also be used as coins. All those zeros can be confusing for first-timers, so make sure you check carefully if you don't want to be short-changed. Credit cards (*carte di credito*) are slowly gaining in popularity, but cash is still preferred in many places.

Banks and private exchange offices throughout the city will change cash and travellers cheques. There are also several ATMs, including those at Banca di Roma in Via Solferino (near Termini), Banca Nazionale del Lavoro at Piazza Risorgimento (near the Vatican) and Deutsche Bank at Largo

Tritone 161 (near the Spanish Steps) which is also the main branch for Visa or MasterCard, should you have any problems with these. If you need money on a Sunday, the Thomas Cook offices at Piazza Barberini 21, Via della Conciliazione 23 and Via del Corso 23 are open in the morning. There are also plenty of private bureaux de change near the popular sights, which are open all day.

Customs regulations

EU nationals do not have to declare goods imported for their personal use. However, European Community law sets out recommended guide levels. Should you exceed these levels, you must be able to show that the goods are for personal use only: 800 cigarettes, 400 cigarillos, 200 cigars, 1kg smoking tobacco, 10 litres spirits, 20 litres fortified wine, 90 litres wine (including maximum 60 sparkling), 110 litres beer.

The current allowances for goods bought duty free by non-EU visitors are: 400 cigarettes or 200 small cigars or 50 cigars or 250g of tobacco; 1 litre of spirits (over 22 per cent alcohol) or 2 litres of fortified wine or 4 litres of table wine; 250ml cologne or 50ml perfume.

For further information on import regulations contact your local HM Customs and Excise Advice Centre or, for Americans, the US Customs Service, PO Box 7407, Washington DC (202) 566 8195.

183

Disabled travellers

Rome does not cater well for travellers with disabilities. Ramps, wide doorways, lifts and modified toilets are rare, although they do exist at Termini station and the Colosseum. With the notable exception of the Vatican Museums (which recently received an EU award for improving accessibility for the disabled), few public buildings have disabled facilities. A number of hotels now claim to offer accommodation for disabled guests, but check any specific requirements before booking. Restaurants are generally helpful, but call in advance to secure the right table. The crowded, cobbled pavements are uneven and often too narrow for wheelchair access and many churches, museums and outdoor archaeological sites have steps to negotiate.

Public transport is also a problem. Not all trains have disabled access (check before you book your journey) and the frequently overcrowded buses and trams can be difficult to use, even though seats at the front are reserved for disabled passengers. However, if you are travelling by car, there are free parking spaces in the city centre (provided you display an official sign), and taxis are relatively inexpensive compared with other capital cities in Europe. If you are travelling unaccompanied, you should perhaps consider a specially-designed package tour or contact an organization for disabled travellers before leaving home. Once in Rome, *CO.IN Via Enrico Giglioli 54a, tel: (06) 23267504, open Mon–Fri 0930–1700* offers help to disabled travellers, and produces a useful guide, *Rome for the Disabled*.

Electricity

The electric current is 220 volts AC, and sockets generally have either two or three round pins. British visitors require an adaptor plug, US visitors a voltage transformer.

Entry formalities

All visitors to Italy require a valid passport. Visas are not required for UK, Eire, American, Canadian, Australian, New Zealand or other EU nationals for stays of under three months. Nationals of most other countries will need a visa, which must be obtained from your nearest Italian embassy or consulate before you travel. Within three days of arrival, all visitors to Italy have to present their passport and register with the police. Most visitors have this formality taken care of by their hotels when they check in. If you are staying elsewhere, you should contact a local police station or the Questura Centrale (the main police station) at Via Genova 2 (*tel: (06) 4686, open 0700–1200*).

Health

No vaccinations are required to enter Italy unless you are coming from a known infected area, but bring mosquito-repellent and sunscreen in the summer. Come prepared for hot weather, with a hat and loose, cool clothing. Drink plenty of fluids and, 'when in Rome' imitate the locals by taking a long lunch break on a shady terrace followed by a siesta.

Rome is famed for its drinking water and its tap water is generally fine to drink. You can even drink from outdoor fountains (unless you see a sign saying *acqua non potabile*). Italians, however, are big mineral water drinkers, so bottled water is widely available.

One of Rome's worst health hazards is the crazy traffic, so be especially vigilant when crossing the road!

Insurance: Should you require medical treatment, EU residents are entitled to the same care as Italians as long as

they have the correct forms – an E111 for British citizens, available through post offices in the UK. These forms cover essential medical treatment, although you will have to pay prescription charges and a percentage of the cost of medicines. They do not provide cover for holiday cancellation, nor do they provide repatriation in case of illness. Private medical insurance is therefore also advisable. Canadian citizens are also covered by a reciprocal arrangement between the Italian and Canadian governments. Other non-EU visitors should take out personal health insurance to cover every eventuality.

Treatment: If you need to visit a doctor, take the E111 form and your passport to the local health office (Unità Sanitaria Locale) who will direct you to a doctor. For emergency treatment, call 113 for an ambulance or go to the nearest casualty department

(*pronto soccorso*) at either Ospedale Fatebenefratelli, Isola Tiberina (*tel: (06) 58731*) or Policlinico Umberto I, Viale Policlinico (*tel: (06) 4462341*). The Rome American Hospital at Via Emilio Longoni 69 (*tel: (06) 22551*) has English-speaking doctors and dentists and the International Medical Centre at Via Giovanni Amendola 7 (*tel: (06) 4882371, nights and weekends (06) 4884051*) also offers a private referral service for English-speaking doctors.

Pharmacies: Farmacie can easily be recognised by a green cross sign. They provide a wide range of prescribed and over-the-counter medicines and drugs and can also offer medical advice on minor ailments. Opening times are usually Mon–Sat 0830–1300, 1600–2000 but local rota systems ensure that at least one pharmacy is open 24 hours a day. Check the rotas posted on the doors. The English-speaking Farmacia Internazionale Capranica at Piazza Capranica 96 and Farmacia Internazionale Barbarini at Piazza Barberini 49 stock American and British pharmaceutical products, while Farmacia della Stazione at Piazza Cinquecento 51 on the corner of Via Cavour (*tel: (06) 4880019*) and Farmacia Piram Omeopatia at Via Nazionale 228 (*tel: (06) 4880754*) are open 24 hours a day, seven days a week.

Information

Tourist offices: The Rome Tourist Office or EPT (*Ente Provinciale per il Turismo di Roma*) is at *Via Parigi 5* (*tel: (06) 48899253, open Mon–Sat*

0815–1915). Other EPT offices are at Fiumicino airport in international arrivals (*tel: (06) 65956074*) and Stazione Termini in front of platform 3 (*tel: (06) 4871270*). Both are open Mon–Sat 0815–1915. For a more friendly and helpful service, try Enjoy Rome, a private agency offering tourist information and accommodation for budget travellers at Via Varese 39 (*tel: (06) 4451843*).

Also dotted around the city near large tourist attractions are a handful of Info-tourism kiosks (*open daily 0900–1800*) containing information on hotels, restaurants, transport, museums and other attractions. You will find them at Largo Goldoni (near the Spanish steps), Piazza San Giovanni in Laterano, Piazza Pia (near Castel Sant' Angelo), Piazza del Tempio della Pace (near the Fori Imperiali), Piazza delle Cinque Lune (near Piazza Navona), Via Nazionale, Stazione Termini, Via dell'Olmata (near Santa Maria Maggiori) and Piazza Sonnino in Trastevere.

The Vatican has its own tourist office (*Ufficio Informazione Pellegrini e Turisti*) on the south side of Piazza San Pietro (*tel: (06) 69884466, open Mon–Sat 0830–1900*).

National Tourist Offices:
Canada: Office National Italien de Tourisme, 1 Place Ville Marie, Suite 1914, Montreal, Quebec H3B 3M9. Tel: (514) 8667667.
Ireland: Italian State Tourist Office, 47 Merrion Square, Dublin 2. Tel: (01) 766397
UK: Italian State Tourist Office, 1 Princes Street, London W1. Tel: (0171) 408 1254.
US: Italian government Tourist Office, 630 5th Avenue, Suite 1565, New York, NY 10111. Tel: (212) 245 4822/3/4.

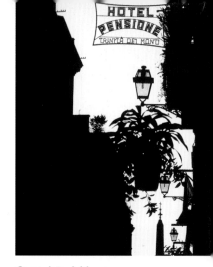

Consulate Addresses:
Australia: Corso Trieste 25C. Tel: (06) 852721.
Canada: Via Zara 30. Tel: (06) 445981.
Ireland: Piazza Campitelli 3. Tel: (06) 6979121.
New Zealand: Via Zara 28. Tel: (06) 4402928.
South Africa: Via Tanaro 14. Tel: (06) 852541.
UK: Via XX Settembre 80A. Tel: (06) 4825441.
US: Via Veneto 121. Tel: (06) 46741.

Useful websites:
http://www.enjoyrome.it/ 'Enjoy Rome's' English-language website offers practical tips and tourist information, especially for young travellers on a strict budget. It also organises walking-tours and bike-tours around the city with English-speaking guides.

http://www.infoRoma.it/romepage.htm Weekly bulletins in English on current events and issues in Rome, including strike warnings!

http://onlinenews.net/Rome.html Useful tips on shopping, sporting events, hotels, business, what's on when, education, food…

http://www.vatican.va/ All you need to know about the Holy See.

Insurance

It is important to take out full health and travel insurance before travelling to Italy (*see Health, page 184*).

Maps

Any tourist office will provide you with a good, free city map and the ATAC kiosk outside Stazione Termini has a map of the main bus and tram routes, also free of charge. For more detailed maps, head for a news stands or a bookstore. Spiral-bound *Roma A–Z* or pocket-sized *Falk Centro di Roma Pianta della Città* are two of the most comprehensive, and include a street index. The official public transport map – *Roma Metro-Bus* – contains detailed street plans, clearly marked transport systems and a booklet listing ticket prices and bus routes.

Opening times

Banks: Most open Mon–Fri 0830–1330. Major branches may also open 1500–1600.

Cafés: Open from early morning (0500 or 0600) until the small hours (typically 0100 or 0200).

Churches: Most open daily 0700–1200 and 1630–1900.

Museums: Museum times vary according to the season and many close on Mondays. See individual entries for details and phone ahead to avoid disappointment.

Post offices: Most open Mon–Fri 0815–1400 and Sat 0815–1200. The main post office in Piazza San Silvestro opens Mon–Fri 0825–2100 and Sat 0800–1200.

Restaurants and bars: Most open from 1230–1500 and 1930–2230 but this may vary slightly from one estabishment to the next. Bars stay open later in the evening. They all have a statutory closing day (*riposo settimanale*) and many close for annual holidays during August.

Shops: Most open from 0900–1300 (fashion stores 1000–1300) and 1600–1900 (1700–2000 in summer), although some stay open all day. They usually close on Monday mornings (except food shops, which close on Thursday afternoons), Sundays and, in many cases, on Saturday afternoons. The shops are less crowded in the mornings as most Romans prefer to shop in the early evening.

Tourist offices: The main EPT Tourist Offices are open Mon–Sat 0815–1915, the information kiosks are open daily 0900–1800 and the Vatican Tourist Office is open Mon–Sat 0830–1900.

Public holidays

1 Jan	New Year's Day
6 Jan	Epiphany
Mar/Apr	Easter Monday
25 Apr	Liberation Day
1 May	Labour Day
29 June	St Peter's Day (Patron saint of Rome)
15 Aug	Assumption
1 Nov	All Saints' Day
8 Dec	Immaculate Conception
25 Dec	Christmas Day
26 Dec	St Stephen's Day

Most shops, museums, banks and businesses close on these days, with the exception of 29 June, when most remain open.

Reading

Newspapers and magazines:
The main European daily newspapers can be bought after 1500 on the day of issue from news stands at Termini, Piazza Colonna, Piazza Navona, Via Vittoria Veneto and near other major tourist sights.

History and art:
The History of the Decline and Fall of the Roman Empire by Edward Gibbon

All of Ancient Rome Then and Now (published by Casa Editrice Bonechi)

Rome – The biography of a City and *The Grand Tour* by Christopher Hibbert

A Traveller in Rome by H V Morton

Art and Architecture in Italy 1600–1750 by Roduol Wittkower

Papal Rome:
The Pope from Poland: An Assessment edited by John Whale

Classical literature and fiction:
The Cambridge History of Classical Literature (Volume II, Latin Literature)

Julius Caesar by William Shakespeare

I, Claudius by Robert Graves

Portrait of a Lady and *Italian Hours* by Henry James

The Woman of Rome and *Roman Tales* by Alberto Moravia

A Violent Life by Pier Paolo Pasolini

History by Elsa Morante

Venus in Copper by Lindsay Davis

Vendetta by Michael Dibdin

Safety and security

As in many cities, petty theft (bag- and necklace-snatching, pickpocketing and car break-ins) is common. Carry all your valuables in a money-belt, not your pockets. Don't put valuables down on a café or restaurant table, wear your camera, sling handbags across the chest and foil scooterised bag-snatchers by walking on the inside of the pavement. Never leave possessions in parked cars and remember to lock the doors. Beware of pickpockets at all times, but especially on crowded buses, at Termini station and in markets. Avoid parks, poorly-lit sidestreets and the area around Termini late at night.

Telephones

Public phones are indicated by a red or yellow sign. They can be found on the street, in most bars and restaurants and in special offices called *Centri Telefoni*, where you speak first and pay later. Phones accept L100, L200 and L500 coins, tokens (*gettoni*) worth L200 and phone cards (*schede telefoniche*), available from post offices, tobacconists and certain bars in L5000 and L10000 denominations. Remember to break off the card's small marked corner before use.

International dialling codes:
From Rome to UK 0044, USA and Canada 001, Australia 0061, New Zealand 0064, Ireland 00353, South Africa 0027.
From outside Italy to Rome 0039 for Italy then 06 for Rome.
Cheap rate for calls is Mon–Sat 2200–0800 and all day Sunday.

Time

Italy is on Central European time (one hour ahead of GMT in winter, two hours in summer).

Tipping

Foreigners are expected to tip more than locals. It is normal to leave L100 or L200 on the counter when buying drinks at the bar and around 10 per cent of the bill in restaurants. However, many of the larger restaurants now include a 10 per cent or 15 per cent service charge on the bill. Keep L1000 or L2000 notes handy for tipping taxi drivers, chambermaids, theatre usherettes, cloakroom attendents and porters.

Toilets

There are fewer than 40 public toilets in Rome, most of them near the major tourist sites, and you have to pay the attendant in order to use them. Alternatively, most bars, hotels, fast food outlets and department stores will let you use their facilities, although they probably won't be as clean as the public ones and they won't necessarily provide toilet paper.

Index

must-see ROME

Editorial, design and production credits

Project management: Dial House Publishing Services
Series editor: Christopher Catling
Copy editor: Sharon Charity
Proof-reader: Posy Gosling

Series and cover design: Trickett & Webb Limited
Cover artwork: Wenham Arts
Text layout: Wenham Arts
Map work: RJS Associates

Repro and image setting: Z2 Repro, Thetford, Norfolk, UK
Printed and bound by: Artes Graficas ELKAR S. Coop., Bilbao, Spain

Picture research: Deborah Emeny